Business Economics

An Introduction

Business Economics

An Introduction

Series Editor
JOSEPH CHILVER

Author
J.T.F. BUTLER

Oxford Business Publishing
Oxford
1991

Business Economics

Published by Oxford Business Publishing
15 King Edward Street
Oxford OX1 4HT

Author's Acknowledgements
I have received considerable assistance and encouragement whilst writing this series of books, and wish to express my particular thanks to:
Stan Hunter, Principal of the Oxford College for Independent Studies, who first conceived the idea for the series, and who has given very generously of his time to ensure that it came to fruition.
Joseph Chilver, Chief Examiner of the Institute of Commercial Management, who read through each of the texts and suggested many improvements and amendments. I am, of course, responsible for any errors which remain.
Fay Luteijn, Registrar of the Oxford College for Independent Studies, who has liaised on my behalf with those who typed the manuscripts, and has brought order to my chaos with good humour and complete unflappability.

ISBN: 1 873234 03 1

Text Design & Typesetting: Electronic Type & Design
Oxford
Cover Design: Steve Flemming, Oxford
Printed and bound in Great Britain by BPCC Hazell Books, Aylesbury, Bucks.

A catalogue record for this book is available from the British Library

Contents

'For D.P'

An Introductory Note

This series of books has been written to precisely meet the needs of students on courses leading to the award of the Institute of Commercial Management's Diploma in Business Studies. Each chapter has been designed to meet the specific needs of the subject syllabus. Including, as they do, an abundance of questions from past papers, the books should prove invaluable to tutors and students involved in these courses.

The texts should also be useful for a wide range of business and management students, including those on BTEC Higher National Diploma and BA Business Studies Degree Courses.

Dr. Joseph Chilver
Series Editor

Foreword

For the past five years the Oxford College for Independent Studies has been preparing students for a wide range of recognised qualifications in preparation for employment or for further study.

During this time the College has used a number of different text books for its courses, but none addressed a specific syllabus; in some instances, too, the details of a given text book would be overwhelming and difficult to assimilate.

Invariably, students would need to carry with them a range of books for each subject under study, and even then not everything for a particular syllabus would be covered.

The College, therefore, set up Oxford Business Publishing and commissioned a series of business texts for its most popular course, the Diploma in Business Studies (Institute of Commercial Management). The series covers eight distinct disciplines of business, and the experience of having taught a wide range of business subjects has enabled the College to prepare the texts with the student in mind.

The Diploma course, in content, is not unlike the BTEC or Higher National Diploma and students studying for either of these qualifications should find the series of books useful. First-year undergraduates, and those embarking on the first levels of professional examinations, should also benefit from one or more of these titles.

S D Hunter
Principal
Oxford College for Independent Studies

1

Introduction to Economics

Objectives

After reading this chapter, you should be able to:

- Understand what is meant by 'scarcity' and 'choice'
- List the primary and secondary factors of production
- Explain what is meant by specialisation
- List the four measures which are important when calculating population growth

Introduction to Economics

Fundamental Concepts

Definitions of Economics

The earliest definitions of economics were in terms of wealth; Adam Smith, for example, whose 'Wealth of Nations' was published in 1776, described his work as 'an inquiry into the nature and causes of the wealth of Nations'. J.S. Mill, writing in the Nineteenth Century, defined economics as 'the practical science of the production and distribution of wealth'. A.C. Pigou's definition of economics emphasised the importance of welfare by suggesting that the subject should study how to increase total production in order to raise living standards. Alfred Marshall defined economics as 'a study of mankind in the ordinary business of life'.

Contemporary economists tend to define economics in terms of 'scarcity' and 'choice'. All goods are considered scarce in the sense that there are not enough of them for everyone to have as much as he would like. Goods are therefore scarce relative to the demand for them. Because of scarcity everyone has to choose between satisfying alternative wants. L. Robbins' definition of economics emphasises scarcity and choice: economics is 'the science which studies human behaviour as a relationship between ends and scarce means which have alternative uses'.

The Exploitation of Resources

As has been shown, the scarcity of resources means that choices have to be made about what to produce, how to produce it, and how to distribute what is produced. Economists call the sum total of the resources available to satisfy human wants 'the factors of production'. The primary factors of production are land and labour: the secondary factors are capital and enterprise. The factors of production are defined below:

- Land includes all the free gifts of nature, such as farmlands, mineral deposits, sunlight and water. Two characteristics of land worth noting are that it is fixed in supply and that it has no cost of production to society.

- Labour includes all the physical and intellectual effort involved in the processes of production.
- Capital includes all the physical assets of society which contribute to the processes of production. Examples of capital are machines and buildings. Two characteristics of capital worth noting are that it is produced by economic activity, and that it results from saving. Capital comes about when an individual decides not to spend all his wealth on consumption, but to save a portion of it, in order to use that portion to increase future production.
- Enterprise is regarded by some economists as a fourth factor of production, because it organises and combines the other factors of production, and because it takes risks by producing goods in anticipation of demand.

All of the factors of production can be regarded as receiving income of one sort or another, which is called factor rewards or factor returns, as the list below shows:

- Land receives Rent
- Labour receives Wages
- Capital receives Interest
- Enterprise receives Profit

Specialisation

A fundamental economic concept is that of specialisation, or the division of labour. Specialisation occurs when individual workers are involved in only part of the productive process, instead of being involved in the whole process. When specialisation occurs, the volume of production increases greatly. Perhaps the most famous example of the effect of division of labour is that provided by Adam Smith in 'The Wealth of Nations'. He observed that one man could produce 20 pins a day if involved in all the processes of production, but that 10 men, each of whom was working on no more than two of the separate processes involved, could produce 48,000 pins a day. According to Smith, division of labour increases production for four main reasons:

- it increases the skill of the work-force, by allowing it to acquire expertise in a narrow range of tasks.
- it saves the time that would be lost when a worker transfers from one task to another.
- it allows an individual to specialise in tasks for which he has a personal aptitude.
- it makes the use of machinery possible as each of the processes of production is separated and clearly defined.

Although modern economic life depends to a very great extent on the increased production resulting from division of labour, this method of production is not without disadvantages, the most important of which are listed below:

- Alienation. When an individual is concerned with only one part of the process of production, he may experience the work as boring or frustrating, and eventually develop feelings of hostility that can become an important underlying cause of industrial relations problems. Modern theories of management attempt to overcome alienation by switching workers from one task to another, and by involving them in the decision making process.
- Specialisation in one field increases dependency on specialists in other fields. This can have important political and economic consequences in international trade, when nations become specialist producers.
- Dislocation. When an economy is highly specialised, and there is great interdependency between industries, problems in one industry can have an adverse effect on other industries.
- Specialisation can make it difficult for workers who are highly skilled in one industry to find alternative employment when their industry declines.

Economics and Population Studies

Economists are concerned with studying population because the relationship between population density and resources provides a good indication of the nature of the future labour supply, as well as showing those areas of the world where food production is of the utmost importance. The table below illustrates how rapidly global population has increased since 1750.

1000 A.D.	300	million
1750	728	million
1987	5000	million

In 1798 the Rev. Thomas Malthus published his 'Essay on the Principle of Population as it Affects the Future Improvement of Society', in which he drew attention to the relationship between population growth and scarce resources. Malthus was aware that the British population was increasing, and saw in this a great danger not only to economic growth but to survival itself. 'Population when unchecked, increases in a geometrical ratio (1,2,4,8,16). Subsistence increases only in an arithmetical ratio (1,2,3,4). A slight acquaintance with numbers will show the immensity of the first power in comparison with the second'. Malthus argued that the pressure of population on resources would increase until population growth was stopped by the 'positive checks' of 'war, pestilence and famine'. After the operation of positive checks, when food once more became available at above-subsistence levels, Malthus assumed that population growth would resume, until similarly stopped in the future.

Although population growth in England has not resulted in the catastrophe predicted by Malthus, some economists believe that Malthus' argument can still be applied to the contemporary world. They argue that population growth in Britain stimulated the development of agricultural improvements in the latter half of the Eighteenth Century, providing the labour which was used to increase production. In the contemporary world, however, there is considerable evidence that without dramatic increases in production, Malthusian positive checks on population will work to decrease excessive population levels. The following table shows a list of countries whose population growth exceeds Gross National Product.

	GNP
1965–84	
Zaire	–1.6
Niger	–1.3
Central African Republic	–0.1
Madagascar	–1.6

Ghana	–1.9
Senegal	–0.5
Zambia	–1.3
El Salvador	–0.6
Nicaragua	–1.5
Peru	–0.1
Jamaica	–0.4
Chile	–0.1
Libya	–0.1

Source: IBRD

Population size is determined by three main factors: the birth-rate, the death-rate and the net figure derived from emigration and immigration. The birth-rate and death-rate are usually expressed per thousand population. Birth-rates and death-rates for various countries are provided in the list below:

	Birth-rate per 1000	
	1965	**1984**
India	45	33
Kenya	51	53
Mexico	45	33
USA	19	16
UK	18	13
France	18	14

Source: IBRD

	Death-rate per 1000	
	1965	**1984**
India	21	12
Kenya	21	13
Mexico	11	7
USA	9	9
UK	12	12

Source: IBRD

It is possible to show the rate at which a population is changing by comparing its death-rate and birth-rate. In 1984, for example, India had a death-rate of 12 per thousand, and a birth-rate of 33 per thousand: its population was therefore increasing at 21 per thousand of population in that year. By contrast the birth-rate in the USA was 16 per thousand, and the death-rate 9, showing an overall increase of 5 per thousand in the same year.

Population growth is also affected by the net reproduction rate (NRR), which measures the number of daughters a new-born girl is likely to bear in her life-time, taking into account fertility and life expectancy. A net reproduction rate of 1 indicates that fertility is at replacement rate.

Other measures which are of importance when calculating population growth are:

- Infant mortality rate: this measures the number of children per thousand of population who die in the first year of life. In India this rate was 90 per thousand in 1984: for the U.K. it was 10 per thousand in the same year.

- Fertility rate: a population can increase if the death-rate declines due to improvements in medicine. It is important for economists to be able to measure the Total Period Fertility Rate, the average number of children borne by women between the ages of 15 and 50. A rate of 2.0 is necessary if the population is to reproduce itself. In 1984 the TPFR for India was 4.6; for Britain it was 1.8.

- Age at marriage and size of family: it is important to know whether the average age at marriage is increasing or decreasing, as this can have important implications for the fertility rate. It is also important to know what non-biological factors influence family size. Social class in many Western nations is a determinant of family size, where it has an inverse relation to size of family.

- Migration: in the mid-Nineteenth Century the population of Ireland declined as a result of emigration. The population increase of the USA in the Nineteenth and early Twentieth Centuries owed much to immigration.

Not only are economists concerned with mere numbers of population; they also wish to know the age and sex distribution of a population, and its geographical and occupational distribution:

- age and sex distribution: this is important because it indicates the size and nature of the work-force, compared to children and old people who are considered to be economically dependent.

- geographical distribution: it is important for economists to identify different densities of population between countries and within regions. In 1984 population per square kilometre in India was 227.9; in England it was 230.0.
- occupational distribution: this shows how the population is distributed between occupations. The industries in which people work are classified as primary (mining, agriculture and fishing), secondary (manufacturing) and tertiary (service industries, education).

The concept of the optimum population is that there is an optimum size and structure of population which contributes to the wealth and welfare of a society. There is no generally applicable formula calculating the optimum population of a specific society, as much depends on the geography and natural resources of the society, and on its technological position. Much depends, also, on its historical development, so that the optimum population for a given society will fluctuate over time.

Summary

1) Contemporary economists tend to define economics from the perspective of scarcity and choice.

2) The factors of production are land, labour, capital and enterprise.

3) The division of labour has four main advantages. It increases the skill of the workforce, saves time, allows individuals to specialise, and makes the use of machinery possible.

4) Population size is due to three factors: the birth-rate, the death-rate and the net figure derived from emigration and immigration.

Self-Assessment Test One – Questions

1) In what sense are goods considered 'scarce' by economists?

2) a) What are the primary factors of production?

b) What are the secondary factors of production?

3) What is meant by 'specialisation'?

4) What four measures are important when calculating population growth?

Self-Assessment Test One – Answers

1) Goods are scare relative to the demand for them.

2) a) Land and labour.

b) Capital and enterprise

3) Division of labour, where an individual performs one part of the productive process instead of all parts.

4) a) birth-rate

b) death-rate

c) infant mortality rate

d) emigration and immigration

Past Examination Questions on These Topics

1) Economics has been defined as 'the science of human behaviour which looks at the relationship between ends and scarce means which have alternative uses'. Explain this definition, and discuss whether or not it is satisfactory.

2) To what extent do you think the key to the problem of many less-developed countries is the control of population growth? What is the effect of the age structure on economic development?

3) Define 'specialisation' and outline its main advantages and disadvantages.

2

Demand and Supply

Objectives

After reading this chapter, you should be able to:

- List the six characteristics of a perfect market
- Explain the circumstances in which demand curves are exceptional
- Explain the circumstances in which supply curves are exceptional
- Define price elasticity of demand, income elasticity of demand and cross elasticity of demand

Demand and Supply

Markets

Perfect and Imperfect Markets.

The function of a market is to facilitate exchange, the buying and selling of goods and services. Economists use the theoretical concept of the 'perfect' market to make analysis of economic activity easier. A perfect market would have the following characteristics:

- Homogeneity of the product or service, so that it makes no difference to the buyer whether he purchases from any one of the sellers.
- A large number of buyers and sellers, so that the market for the product or service cannot be influenced by the actions of individual buyers or sellers.
- Buyers and sellers are in close contact with one another, so that changes in the supply or demand for the product or service are known to all participants.
- No preferential treatment, in the way of discounts or duties imposed on purchases or sales.
- Free movement into and out of the market, so that people can decide whether they wish to begin trading in the product or service, or cease trading.
- The product or service is easily transferable.

The underlying principle of the perfect market is that prices are determined solely by the interaction of demand and supply. Although the perfect market remains a theoretical concept some markets come quite close to meeting the conditions of perfection listed above. In the Stock Exchange, for example, the price of shares is known to all participants, each share in a company is identical, the ownership of shares is readily transferable, and buyers and sellers base their actions solely on the price of shares. One of the reasons why the Stock Exchange cannot be considered a truly perfect market, however, is that knowledge of the present price alone is not enough to justify a decision to buy or sell shares.

Most markets in the real world are imperfect. In the retail market, for example, buyers are not in close contact with each other, and sometimes fail to make purchases at the lowest price because they do not know which retail outlet is selling at the lowest price. Similarly, the decision to purchase at a specific retail outlet may have more to do with habit or convenience, than with the price of products. The market in houses is seriously imperfect, because houses cannot be transported from one part of the country to another. Any market subject to government intervention in the form of import duties, taxes or subsidies, is thereby made imperfect. The most important characteristic of an imperfect market is that similar products in it can be sold at different prices.

Economists recognise the existence of a wide variety of markets, the most significant of which are listed below:

– Factor markets, in which the services of each of the four factors are purchased.

– Consumer goods markets, sometimes called markets for final products: these are sub-divided into wholesale and retail markets.

– Capital market for new securities.

– Stock Exchange market for existing securities.

– Money market for short-term loans.

– Foreign exchange market for foreign currencies.

Wholesale Marketing

Most manufacturers prefer to sell their products in bulk at the point of manufacture, rather than become involved in the separate business of distributing small quantities to individual retailers. The first function of the wholesaler is to receive large product quantities from the manufacturer, and to divide these into smaller quantities for distribution to the retailer.

Wholesalers provide warehousing and storage facilities for manufacturers, and contribute to product price stability by releasing their stocks onto the market in a planned and regular way. Wholesalers sometimes assist manufacturers and retailers in marketing a product, by passing on information from retailers to manufacturers. Wholesalers also provide expert knowledge of certain products, and can prepare products for sale. In some circumstances wholesalers can also provide finance for retailers, thus enabling manufacturers to receive prompt payment for their products, and retailers to obtain credit facilities or discounts on purchases.

The wholesaling of many commodities takes place in highly organised markets, where buyers and sellers meet together in order to conduct their business. Such markets have quite a high degree of perfection, because the contact between buyers and sellers ensures that the price of the commodity remains the same throughout the market. Highly organised markets come into existence when the following conditions are met:

- the commodity must be durable, so that large quantities of it can be held in stock.
- it is helpful if the price of the commodity is liable to wide short-term fluctuations because of the difficulty of increasing or decreasing the supply.

Examples of commodities which meet these two conditions are: wheat, tea, coffee, sugar, cotton, wool, lead, tin, copper and timber.

Where a commodity's quality can be reliably graded, as in the case of cotton and wheat, the buyer does not have to inspect his potential purchase, and exchange usually takes the form of private treaty. Where the commodity's quality cannot be graded, however, buyers take samples of the product, which is then usually sold at auction.

The grading of commodities allows for the development of futures markets, a 'future' being a contract to deliver a consignment of the commodity at a future date at an agreed price. In a futures market the 'spot' price is the price for immediate delivery. A merchant who believes the 'spot' price of cotton is likely to rise in the short-term, will buy futures if he can obtain them at a lower price than what he thinks will be the market price, as a hedge against a rise in the cotton price. A manufacturer whose commodity cannot be bought in the market immediately can insure himself against a possible future price fall by selling futures in order to obtain the current price. The existence of futures markets in commodities compensates for wide fluctuations in prices, and thus brings markets closer to perfection.

Demand and Supply

Demand for a product or service means the quantity demanded at a certain price. As a general rule the quantity demanded of a product will fall if the price rises, and increase if the price falls.

Demand Schedules and Curves

A consumer's demand for a product is dependent on the price of the product. An individual demand schedule, such as the one below, illustrates how demand for a product increases as the price of the product falls. Consumer A is willing to buy one tin of sardines if the price per tin is 48 pence, but 5 tins if the price per tin is 35 pence.

Consumer A

Sardines: price per tin	**Quantity Demanded**
48	1
46	2
41	3
40	3
37	4
35	5

Consumer B, on the other hand, will not purchase sardines until the price falls to 41 pence per tin, and instead of buying five tins at 35 pence each, will buy only 3 tins.

Consumer B

Sardines: price per tin	**Quantity Demanded**
48	0
46	0
41	1
40	2
37	3
35	3

A composite demand schedule is a theoretical combination of all the individual demand schedules for a specific product. It represents the total demand for the product at different prices. A total demand schedule for sardines might look like this:

Total Demand Schedule

Sardines: Price per tin	**Quantity Demanded**
48	1,000
46	1,000
41	2,000
40	2,000
37	3,000
35	4,000

A demand schedule can be expressed in a graph, as the example below shows. It is a convention in economics that the horizontal axis is marked OX, and the vertical OY: it is also conventional to show price along the vertical scale, and quantity along the horizontal. In this example of a demand curve the curve DD shows the state of demand for sardines at different prices. As the purpose of the demand curve is merely to show the relationship between price and the quantity bought, there is no need for the price and quantity scales to be marked off mathematically. The graph may be drawn thus:

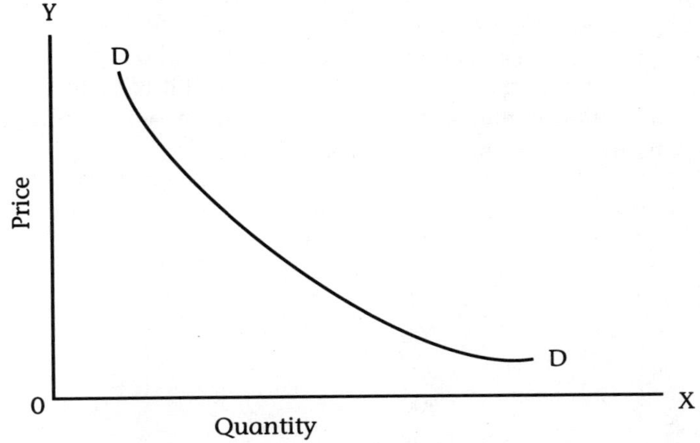

This graph illustrates the First Law of Supply and Demand: the lower the price, the greater the quantity that will be demanded.

Most demand curves follow the slope of the one shown above, but some exceptional demand curves slope upwards from left to right before moving down, showing that demand increases as the price rises, instead of decreasing as the price rises. Exceptional demand curves occur in the following conditions:

- Luxury goods: demand for some luxury goods increases as prices rise, as they are seen as more desirable. Perfume is an example of this.
- Fear of price rises: if it is feared that price rises are imminent, despite a recent price rise, demand may increase; this happens frequently on the Stock Exchange.
- Inferior goods: cheap staple foods are a good example of exceptional demand. Quantities bought do not vary that greatly over quite wide price ranges. But when prices generally are rising, the quantity of cheap staple foods demanded may increase as the price of other foods moves beyond the reach of the very poor.

Supply Schedules and Curves.

Just as there is a relationship between demand and price, so there is a relationship between supply and price. Supply indicates the willingness of producers to sell their products in greater or lesser quantities, according to price. It is a general rule that sellers will be willing to supply more of a product if the price is rising, and less if it is falling. The table below illustrates a supply schedule for sardines, showing the quantities that will be put on the market at different prices:

Sardines: Price per tin	**Quantity Supplied**
48	4,000
46	3,500
41	3,000
40	2,000
37	1,500
35	1,000

In this example 4,000 tins of sardines will be put on the market if the price reaches 48 pence a tin, but only 1,000 tins will be offered if the price falls to 35 pence per tin. This illustrates the Second Law of Supply and Demand: the higher the price, the greater the quantity that will be supplied.

A supply schedule can also be represented graphically:

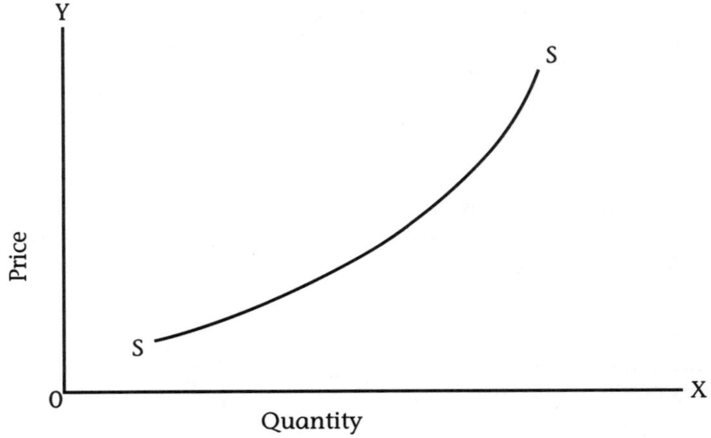

Exceptional supply curves occur in the following circumstances:

- the supply of some products is fixed, because of their rarity; works of art are an example of products falling into this category. If the supply of a product is fixed, then an increase in price will not result in a greater quantity of the product being offered for sale.
- the supply curve for labour may sometimes slope backwards on a portion of the curve, as a work-force is prepared to work less hours if wages are high.

The Equilibrium of Demand and Supply

The price at which demand and supply are equal is known as the equilibrium price. At this price the quantity demanded will be equal to the quantity supplied. The equilibrium price for sardines can be found by combining the demand and supply schedules:

Combined Demand and Supply Schedule

Sardines	**Quantity**	
Price per tin	**Demanded**	**Supplied**
48	1,000	4,000
46	1,000	3,500
41	2,000	3,000
40	2,000	2,000
37	3,000	1,500
35	4,000	1,000

The equilibrium price for sardines in this example is therefore 40 pence per tin, because at this price demand and supply will both be 2,000 tins. This can be represented graphically as is shown below: the equilibrium price on the graph is OP, at which price the quantity OQ

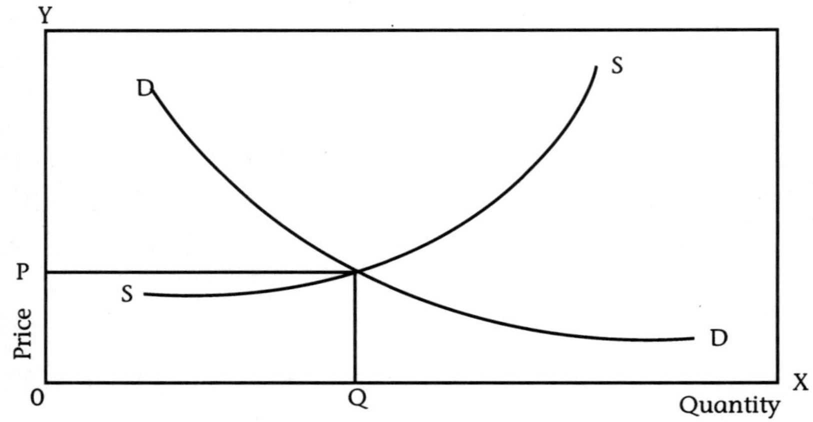

will be supplied. If the equilibrium price of a product is the price actually charged for the product in the market, there will be a sufficient quantity supplied to meet demand at that price.

If the market price is higher than the equilibrium price, then some quantity of the product will remain unsold. If the market price is lower than the equilibrium price, then there will be a shortage of the product, as demand at that price exceeds supply. The determination of price by the interaction of supply and demand is known as the price mechanism.

Demand and Supply Relationships

Changes in Demand

Before considering the effect of changes in demand, it is important to note the distinction between movement along a demand curve, and shifts in demand. In the graph below, which shows a demand curve, the quantity of goods demanded varies according to the price of the goods. This does not show a change in demand, but merely a

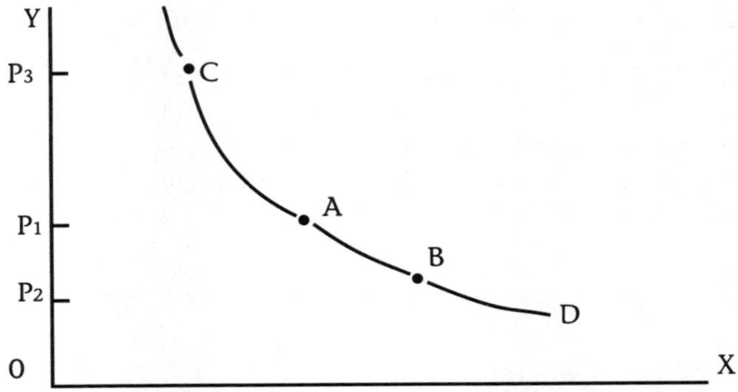

movement along the same demand curve. In the next graph, however, demand has increased. A greater quantity of the product is now being demanded at the old prices. If demand had declined the new curve D2 would be to the left of the original curve D1. At the

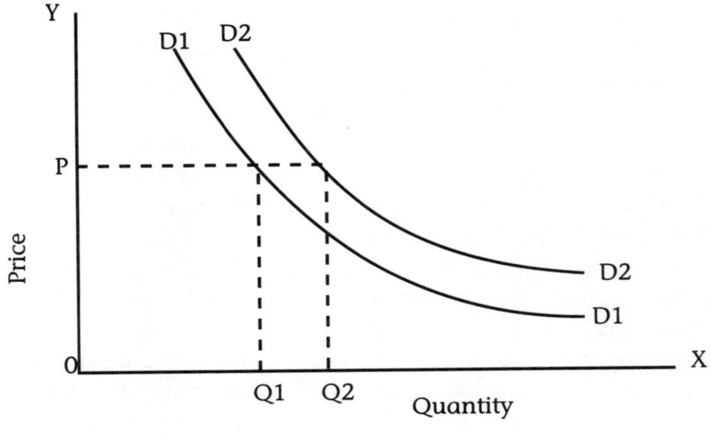

price OP demand has shifted from OQ1, to OQ2.

The following are some of the most important causes of changes in demand:

- Increases in real income: this will usually cause an increase in demand for luxury items and consumer durables, although it may have little effect on the demand for basic foodstuffs and necessities.
- Changes in the quantity of money: an increase or decrease in the quantity of money will affect demand, as the prices of goods will not change in the same proportion as the increase or decrease in the quantity of money.
- Changes in income distribution: government policies on taxation, public expenditure, and subsidies to basic foodstuffs affect demand by re-distributing income.
- Changes in population: an increase in total population will increase the demand for food, housing and power. Age distribution is important here, as an increase in the proportion of young people in a population will increase demand in those markets established to meet the wants of young people, eg clothes, records and leisure products.
- Changes in taste or fashion: clothing, food, and entertainment are all subject to changes in demand resulting from changes in taste or fashion.
- Changes in the price of other commodities: some products, like petrol and cars, are complementary: an increase in the price of one causes demand for both products to decrease. Some products are substitutes for others, such as rail and bus travel: increased demand for railway travel due to a fall in price, may be accompanied by a decrease in demand for bus travel.

Changes in Supply

The same distinction between movements along the same supply curve, and shifts in supply, has to be observed as in the case of demand. In the graph below, supply has increased at the price OP, from OQ1, to OQ2.

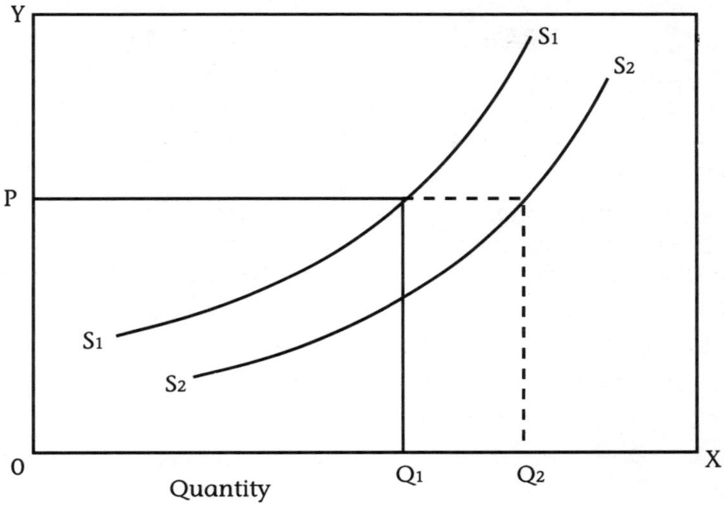

The following are some of the most important causes of changes in supply:

- Changes in the average costs of production: where the cost of raw materials increases, supply will decrease. Where technological improvements reduce the average costs of production, supply will increase.
- Effects of the weather: in agricultural industries output can be affected by weather conditions, making it very difficult to estimate total production in advance. Supply responses to price changes in agriculture are slow, because of the long period between seed-time and harvest.
- Changes in taxation: an increase in the tax on a commodity will generally decrease supply, as such a tax is similar to a rise in the average cost of production.
- Changes in the price of other commodities: if the price of certain commodities rises, the supply of other commodities may fall as producers divert resources to those commodities whose prices are rising.

Effects of Changes in Demand and Supply.

The following are the main effects of changes in demand:

- If demand increases, the effect in the short-term before supply has increased in response to the greater demand, will be for prices to rise. An increase in demand therefore tends to increase both the price and the quantity supplied.
- If demand decreases, there is a tendency for both the price and quantity supplied to decrease.

The following are the main effects of changes in supply:

- If supply increases, there is a tendency for the price to decrease and the quantity demanded to increase.
- If supply decreases, there is a tendency for the price to increase and the quantity demanded to decrease.

Elasticity

Price Elasticity of Demand

The elasticity of demand is a measure of the responsiveness of demand to changes in price. If a small change in price causes a large change in demand, demand is elastic: if a large change in price has only a small effect on demand, demand is relatively inelastic. If demand is perfectly elastic, the demand curve will be horizontal: if

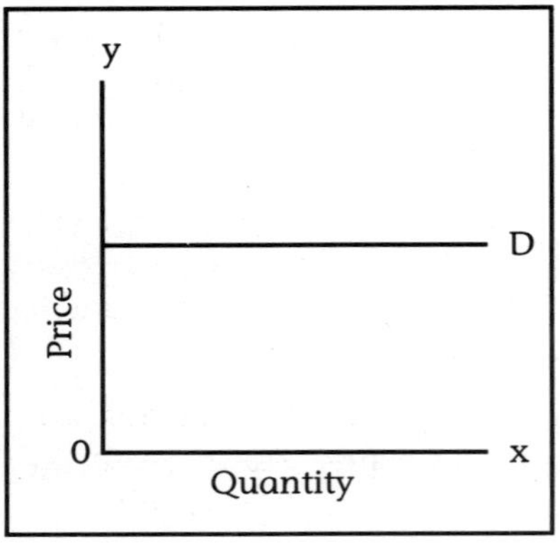

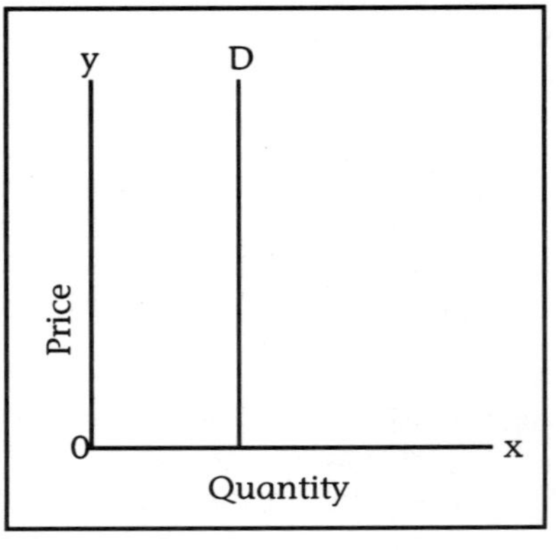

demand is perfectly inelastic, the demand curve will be vertical.

Most demand curves fall somewhere between these two extremes, and also demonstrate different elasticities over different parts of their lengths. This is shown in the large graph below.

Price elasticity of demand is calculated thus:

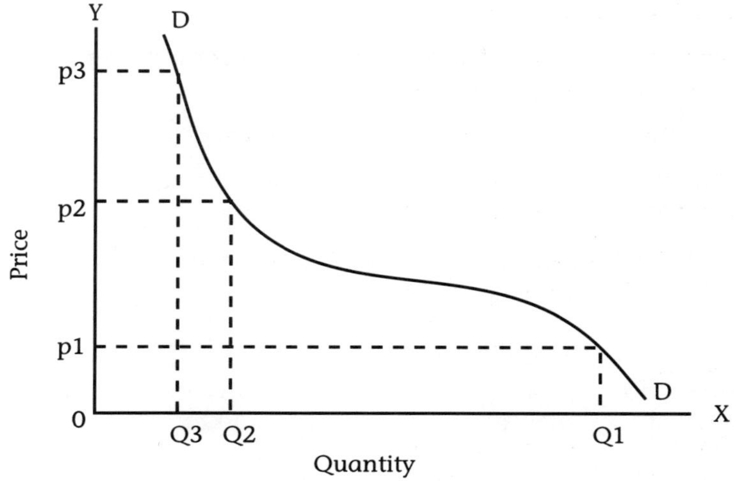

$$\text{Price elasticity of demand} = \frac{\text{\% change in Quantity demanded}}{\text{\% change in price}}$$

Where elasticity of demand is greater than 1, demand is elastic. Where it is equal to 1, there is said to unit elasticity. Where it is less than one, demand is inelastic.

The following factors influence elasticity of demand:

- Substitutes: where substitutes for a product are available, demand for the product tends to be fairly elastic as consumers can respond to price increases by switching to the substitute products.
- Income: the higher an individual's income, the more inelastic his demand is likely to be, as price increases are not felt so much. In the same way the demand for very cheap items is generally inelastic.

- Habit: demand for products which are habit-forming, such as alcohol and tobacco, tends to be inelastic.
- Durability: the demand for durable goods tends to be fairly elastic, as consumers take advantage of a fall in prices to replace television sets or cars.

Income Elasticity of Demand

Income elasticity of demand is a calculation of the responsiveness of demand to changes in income. A low income elasticity of demand indicates that demand is not very responsive to changes in real or disposable income. A high income elasticity of demand indicates that demand is responsive to changes in disposable or real income. Income elasticity of demand is calculated thus:

$$\text{Income elasticity of demand} = \frac{\text{\% change in quantity demanded}}{\text{\% change in income}}$$

Cross Elasticity of Demand

In the case of commodities which are substitutes for one another, a rise in the price of one will cause a rise in demand for the other. Cross elasticity of demand is a measurement of the responsiveness of demand for one product to a change in the price of another. It is calculated thus:

$$\text{Cross elasticity of demand} = \frac{\text{\% change in quantity demanded of product A}}{\text{\% change in price of product B}}$$

Note that although cross elasticity of demand is high between substitute products such as apples and pears, it is negative between complementary products such as petrol and cars.

Elasticity of Supply

The elasticity of supply is a measure of the responsiveness of supply to changes in price. If a change in price causes a less then proportionate change in supply, then supply is relatively inelastic : if a change in price causes a more than proportionate change in supply, then supply is relatively elastic. If supply is perfectly inelastic, the supply curve will be vertical: is supply is perfectly elastic, the supply curve will be horizontal.

Most supply curves fall somewhere between these two extremes, and also demonstrate different elasticities over different parts of their

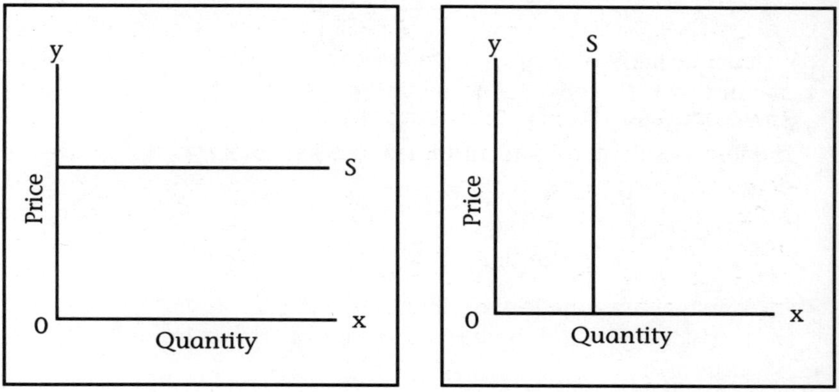

lengths. This is shown in the graph below:

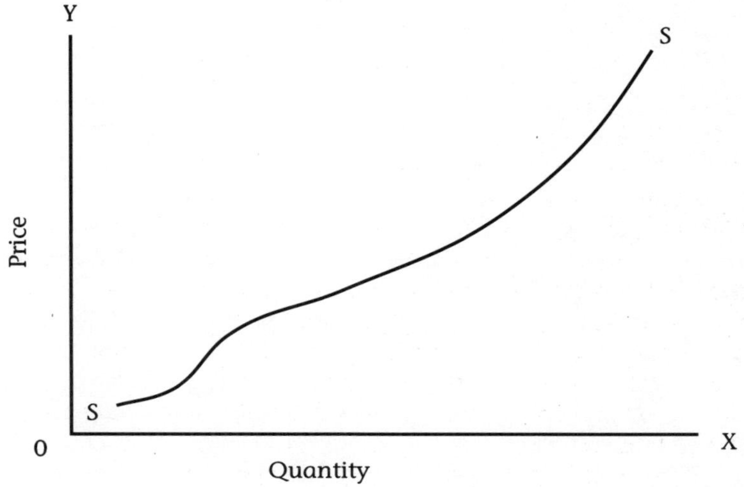

Elasticity of supply is calculated thus:

$$\text{Elasticity of supply} = \frac{\text{\% change in quantity supplied}}{\text{\% change in price}}$$

Where elasticity of supply is greater than 1, supply is elastic. Where it is equal to 1, there is said to be unit elasticity. Where it is less than 1, supply is inelastic.

The following factors influence elasticity of supply:

- Time: the longer it takes to produce a commodity, the less responsive to price changes will the supply of the commodity be. The supply of raw materials and agricultural products tends to be inelastic.
- Factors of production: an increase in supply in response to price rises is made difficult if there is a shortage of labour, land, capital or enterprise.
- Supply is increased by an expansion of output by existing firms, or by the entry into the market of new firms. Supply is reduced by a contraction of output, or when firms leave the market. Elasticity of supply depends on the ease with which supply can be increased or decreased in response to price changes.

Summary

1) The six characteristics of a perfect market are: homogeneity of product or service, large number of buyers and sellers, buyers and sellers in close contact, no preferential treatment, free entry and egress of the market, and easily transferable product or service.

2) Exceptional demand curves occur in luxury goods, inferior goods, and when consumers fear the imposition of higher prices. Exceptional supply curves occur when supply is fixed because of product rarity and when workers work less hours as a result of an increase in wages.

3) Price elasticity of demand is a measure of the responsiveness of demand to changes in price. Income elasticity of demand is a measure of the responsiveness of demand to changes in income. Cross elasticity of demand is a measure of the responsiveness of demand for one product to a change in the price of another.

Self-Assessment Test Two – Questions

1) What are the six characteristics of a perfect market?

2) What are the two conditions necessary for the development of highly organised markets?

3) In what three circumstances do exceptional demand curves occur?

4) In what two circumstances do exceptional supply curves occur?

5) Define:

a) price elasticity of demand

b) income elasticity of demand

c) cross elasticity of demand

Self-Assessment Test Two – Answers

1) a) homogeneity of product or service

b) large number of buyers and sellers

c) buyers and sellers in close contact

d) no preferential treatment

e) free entry and egress of the market

f) product or service is easily transferable

2) a) commodity must be durable

b) price of the commodity liable to wide short-term fluctuations.

3) a) luxury goods

b) fear of price rises

c) inferior goods

4) a) where supply is fixed because of the rarity of the product.

b) the supply curve for labour may sometimes slope backwards on a portion of its curve, as a workforce reduces its hours of work in response to higher wages.

5) a) measure of the responsiveness of demand to changes in price.

b) measure of the responsiveness of demand to changes in income.

c) measure of the responsiveness of demand for one product to a change in the price of another.

Past Examination Questions on These Topics

1) Explain the term 'price elasticity of demand' and show how it can be significant in making economic decisions.

2) 'The supply of houses is increasing, but house prices are rising.' With the help of diagrams, explain this apparent contradiction of economic theory.

3) With the use of appropriate diagrams, explain the likely effect on the demand for and supply of bricks, of the following:

a) a considerable and prolonged fall in the price of houses.

b) an increase in real incomes.

c) improved techniques in the brick-making industry.

4) Explain the terms:

a) price elasticity of demand

b) income elasticity of demand

5) Outline and comment upon any theory which helps to explain why more of a commodity will normally be demanded at a lower price than at a higher price.

6) Explain, with the aid of diagrams, how the price of a commodity is determined in a freely competitive market. Show how the price is affected by:

a) a tax on the commodity

b) a government subsidy on each unit to the producers

7) Given a competitive market situation, discuss what is meant by the price equilibrium intersection. Illustrating your answer with annotated diagrams, show the variations of the equilibrium point resulting from:

a) a specific tax imposed by the government on a commodity.

b) a new cheaper substitute entering the market.

8) Distinguish between price elasticity of demand and income elasticity of demand. Illustrate by reference to particular commodities.

9) Explain precisely what is meant by:

a) price elasticity of demand

b) income elasticity of demand

Give two examples of the use of each of these concepts in economic decision-making.

10) a) Define 'price elasticity of demand'.

b) The following is the demand schedule for good X. Between which price range is demand elastic? Explain why.

Price pence	Quantity demanded
20	220
30	200
40	180
50	170
60	100
70	90

c) Define income elasticity of demand.

d) Why would a firm which is planning its future output capacity be interested in the income elasticity of demand for its products?

11) Define:

a) price elasticity of demand

b) price elasticity of supply

c) income elasticity of demand

3

Production

Objectives

After reading this chapter, you should be able to:

- Describe the two main advantages of public enterprises
- Distinguish between internal and external economies of scale
- List the most important influences on the location of industry
- Describe the main advantages of the localisation of industry

Production

The Organisation of Business

The Sole Proprietor

The oldest and most common type of business unit in Britain is that of the sole proprietor or trader. Many sole proprietors employ staff, but the term 'sole trader' indicates that control of the firm is the responsibility of one person, who owns the capital resources of the business, and to whom any profits from the business also accrue. Most businesses of this type are relatively small. The main advantages of this business structure are:

- Self-interest is a powerful motive for success in the running of a small business, where the rewards for effort go directly to the owner of the business.
- The sole proprietor can make managerial decisions without having to consult others, and can ensure that his decisions are implemented immediately. This makes the business very responsive to changes in market conditions.
- The sole proprietor of a small business has personal contact with both customers and staff members, which makes it easier for him to understand and respond to customer and staff needs, than it is for managers in a large firm.

The main disadvantages of this kind of business are:

- A sole proprietor may find it difficult to acquire sufficient capital to finance expansion of the business.
- The success of the business depends very much on the personality and expertise of the owner of the business. Many sole traders who are very skilled in the kind of product or service they are offering, nevertheless fail because they have no aptitude for business itself.
- A sole proprietor is personally liable for the debts and financial obligations of the firm.

The Partnership

There are two types of partnership, the ordinary partnership and the limited partnership. A partnership is defined as a group of people who carry on business with the purpose of making a profit. A partnership is normally formed by the partners drawing up a Deed of Partnership Agreement which contains the following information:

- Names of the partners.
- Amount of capital contributed by each partner.
- Basis on which profits and losses are to be distributed among the partners.

In a partnership all the partners have equal powers and responsibilities so that;

- each partner may bind the firm in any contract made on behalf of the partnership.
- each partner has the right to take an active role in the management of the firm.
- all the partners are jointly liable for the debts of the firm.

The main advantages of this kind of business are:

- A partnership increases the amount of capital available to a business.
- A partnership allows individual partners to contribute their personal skills and expertise to the management of the business.
- Business decisions can still be made quickly, and the partners are in close contact both with each other and with customers and staff members.

The main disadvantages of this kind of business are:

- In ordinary partnerships there is no limited liability, so that the partners are responsible for the debts of the firm. In a limited partnership only one partner need bear this risk, but the other partners lose their right to take part in the management of the business.
- A partner with poor business acumen may bind the other partners in unwise trading contracts.

- The consent of all the partners is required before new partners may be admitted to the firm, and this can cause problems when personality clashes inhibit the expansion of the firm through the introduction of new partners.

Limited Companies

The development of the partnership came about because of the need for sole proprietors to increase the amount of capital available for their businesses. Joint-stock companies came about to further increase the amount of capital available for businesses. In a joint-stock company members of the company invest in it by buying shares, and control of the company is through shareholder's meetings. A very significant aspect of joint-stock companies is the principle of limited liability, by which shareholders are liable for the debts or obligations of the company only to the extent of their shareholdings.
Limited companies are of two main kinds:

- private companies: the shareholders have limited liability and shares may not be offered for sale to the public. Most private limited companies are family concerns.
- public companies: in addition to the shareholders having limited liability, the following characteristics of the public company should be noted:
  - shares are freely transferable and may be bought and sold on a Stock Exchange
  - the public can be asked to subscribe capital

The main advantages of public companies are:

- Very large amounts of capital can be raised, which assists production on a large scale.
- The public company exists as a legal person, independently of its members.
- Shareholders are protected by limited liability.
- Shareholders may buy and sell shares on a Stock Exchange.

The main disadvantages of public companies are:

- Employees may feel alienated from the interests and activities of public companies, if the companies are very large.

- Investors are principally interested in securing a good return on their capital, and may take little interest in other company matters.

Co-operative Retail Societies

Producers' co-operatives have not been very successful in Britain historically, although there are signs that this may be changing. In this form of business the workers themselves own the business, and elect or appoint managers. The co-operative movement has a three-tiered structure, consisting of:

- Local retail societies, which have branches throughout an area selling groceries and meat.
- The Co-operative Wholesale Society, which makes bulk purchases from grocers and manufacturers, and distributes these stocks to the retail societies. Dividends are payable to the retail societies on the basis of their purchases.

The main advantages of this kind of business are:

- the creation of a private market made up of members.
- the societies provide social, educational and welfare facilities for members and their families.

The main disadvantages of this kind of business are:

- many societies are too small to take advantage of the benefits available from bulk buying and centralised management control.
- there is a tendency for members to withdraw their share capital when economic conditions decline, and this can threaten the stability of the co-operative organisation.

State Enterprises

During the period 1945-1951 many private enterprises were taken over by the government, as it was thought better that the running of them should not be left to free enterprise. The nationalisation programme of this period saw the following industries taken over in this way: the Bank of England, coal-mining, gas and electricity. By 1967 the list of nationalised industries had grown to include: British Rail, London Transport, British Waterways, and the British Iron and Steel Corporation. A nationalised industry has its chairman appointed by the Minister of the appropriate government

department, and is required to prepare and submit an annual report to the Minister. (It should be noted that in the period 1979-1990 many previously nationalised industries became public companies, under the 'privatisation' programme of the Conservative government. Industries thus returning to the public sector included British Gas, British Telecom and British Waterways).
The main advantages of public enterprises are:

- Nationalisation allows the development of an industry to be planned at the centre.
- Nationalised industries do not have to maximise profits as their first concern, but may set themselves social objectives.

The following are the main disadvantages of public enterprises:

- Nationalised industries tend to be very large and adopt bureaucratic forms to control.
- Nationalised industries tend to be monopolies, and therefore do not have to compete with rival firms in order to sell their products and services.
- Nationalised industries which are inefficient are kept in existence by subsidies which are paid for out of taxation.

The Scale of Production

The Tendency to Expand

Production is carried on by a large number of firms of different sizes and types, which may be sole traders, partnerships, large public companies and state enterprises. An industry consists of all the firms of various sizes and kinds which produce broadly similar commodities.

It is the aim of every producer to maximise profits, and therefore it is assumed that a producer will adopt that form of production where costs are lowest; economists assume that there is a tendency for firms to expand as producers seek economies of scale.

Large scale production has been made possible in developed countries as a result of specialisation, improvements in transportation systems, and the capital made available to public companies by shareholders. Increased production has been accompanied in these countries by increased demand as living standards have risen.

Economies of Scale

Economies of scale resulting from increased production are of two kinds: those which can be achieved by a single firm, and those which can be achieved by the increased production of a whole industry. The former are known as internal economies of large scale production, whilst the latter are known as external economies of large scale production.
Examples of internal economies of scale include:

- Economies in the use of factors of production: an increased output at a lower cost per unit of production than was achieved with a lower output, is obtainable with economies affecting the use of land, labour or capital.
- Economies in administration: as a firm expands, it can afford to invest in office machinery and computer equipment to keep the cost of administration to a minimum.
- Marketing economies: a large firm can buy raw materials in bulk, and receive discounts for doing so; a small firm cannot afford to make bulk purchases. Selling costs are also reduced for a large firm, which can advertise its products nationally, where a small firm can afford only local advertising.
- Financial economies: a large firm can benefit from preferential interest rates when borrowing from banks, where a small firm may not be able to secure preferential interest rates on loans.
- Research and development: a large firm can keep abreast of changes in the product market by establishing technical and marketing research departments.

Examples of external economies of scale include:

- Regional division of labour: an industry which develops in a particular area will allow individual firms to specialise in single processes, which increases total output and reduces the average cost of production.

- A supply of skilled labour: an industry which develops in a particular area will develop a pool of labour skills from which all the firms involved in the industry benefit.
- Provision of common services: when an industry expands, common services are frequently developed, such as transport, banking and research facilities.

The Limits to Expansion

Although a firm can achieve economies of scale by expansion in the ways outlined above, a number of factors inhibit the infinite expansion of firms. These factors are considered below:

- The market: obviously a firm cannot expand beyond the market's demand for its product or services. The extent of the demand for a commodity has a greater effect on industries than it does on individual firms.
- Individuality and standardisation: mass production usually results in the standardisation of a product, and although economies of scale can be achieved by mass production, consumer demand for customised products may limit the demand for standardised products.
- Some firms may be inhibited from expanding because of the difficulties of raising capital.
- Increased risk: as the scale of production increases, so do the risks of production. Some owners do not expand because they do not wish to meet the increased risks involved.

In addition to the above factors which inhibit the expansion of firms, it is important to note the following disadvantages of large scale production:

- Bureaucracy: large firms rely to a great extent on bureaucratic forms of control and this can lead to organisational inefficiency.
- Response to change: large firms can be resistant to change, or respond slowly to change.
- Whereas the interests of a sole proprietor and that of the firm can be assumed to be the same it frequently happens in large organisations that there is a disparity between the interests of organisation members and the formal objectives of the organisation.

Vertical and Horizontal Integration

Expansion also occurs when two or more firms amalgamate. Vertical integration is a form of amalgamation in which different stages of production are brought under single control. A manufacturer may integrate by acquiring control of the source of his raw materials, or integrate by acquiring control of the distribution of his products. Horizontal integration is a form of amalgamation in which firms engaged in the same stages of production are brought under single control.

The Law of Diminishing Returns

The Law of Diminishing Returns states that if one or more factors used in a form of production is fixed, and increasing amounts of other factors are combined with the fixed factor or factors, then both the average output in relation to the variable factor, and successive additions to total output, will eventually diminish. If the Law of Diminishing Returns did not exist with regard to farming, for example, it would be possible to increase the yield of any one farm infinitely, by increasing the factors of labour, capital and enterprise engaged in production on it. The graph below illustrates the Law of Diminishing Returns as it might apply to a farm, where the fixed factor is land, and the variable factor is labour.

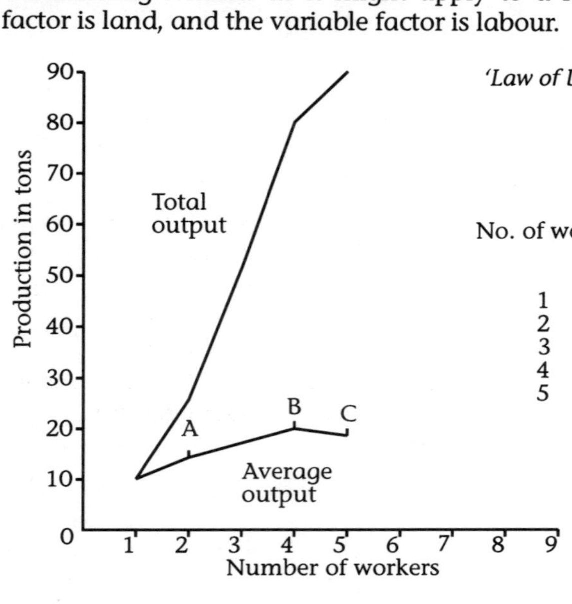

'Law of Diminishing Returns'

No. of workers	Output	Average Output
1	10	10
2	25	12.5
3	51	17
4	80	20
5	90	18

It can be seen from the graph that at point A, production has increased with the acquisition of one worker, and that it continues to increase until point B: from point B to C, however, average production per additional worker declines.

The Location of Industry

The fundamental principle underlying the location of industry is that the production of a commodity tends to be located where it can be carried on at lowest cost. Some of the most important influences on the location of industry are:

- Land: the closer land is to the centre of a city or town, the more expensive it tends to be, as there are more users competing for it.
- Power: in the early days of the Industrial Revolution industries which required a power supply tended to be sited near water or coal deposits; nowadays power is more easily available than in the past.
- Proximity to raw materials: it makes economic sense for an industry which relies on a large supply of raw materials to be located near its source of raw materials, rather than to incur the costs of transporting raw materials a long distance.
- Labour: every industry requires a suitable supply of labour; suitability encompasses not only skills and experience of certain sorts of work, but industrial relations behaviour as well. An industry will be reluctant to locate itself in an area of high unemployment if the local population has a bad record of absenteeism or labour disputes.
- Markets: as well as being located near its supply of raw materials and labour, an industry also needs to be located within reasonable distance of its markets, to avoid the cost of transporting its finished products long distances. Relatively cheap but heavy commodities, such as bricks, are usually manufactured near their markets, but expensive products which are cheap to transport may be manufactured a long way away from their market.

Sometimes a government will have social policies which become important influences on the location of industry. The localisation of an industry can make a district dependent upon the prosperity of that industry, and successive governments have intervened in various ways to affect the location of industry. The following are the main advantages of the localisation of industry:

- Supply of skilled labour: localisation makes it easier for new firms to establish themselves in the industry, as there is a pool of skilled labour from which they can benefit.
- Regional division of labour: when an industry is localised it becomes possible for individual firms to specialise in one or more of the processes of production, thus increasing the total output of the industry.
- Development of subsidiary industries: localisation encourages the development of subsidiary industries which fulfill the needs of the major industry.
- Organised markets: localisation encourages the development of organised markets, such as the Liverpool Cotton Exchange.

The following are the main disadvantages of the localisation of industry:

- Unemployment: if an industry is localised, and demand for its product declines, or improvements in technology mean that fewer workers are required, the unemployment rate of entire districts can cause social and political problems.
- Urban concentration: the localisation of industry can result in the growth of large conurbations which become dependent on the prosperity of the industry.

The Distribution of Industry and of Population

In Britain there is a clear relationship between the location of industry and the distribution of population. There has been a substantial shift in the geographical distribution of the population from the north to the south of England in the Twentieth Century. As the importance of coal declined as a factor influencing the location of industry, firms began to establish themselves near their markets, instead of near their supply of power or raw materials: the car industry, light engineering and rayon cloth manufacture were all established in the south of the country, and drew workers from the older industrial centres of the north. The table below illustrates the shift in the geographical distribution of the population during the period 1961–1981:

Population in 000's

	1961	**1971**	**1981**
North England	3250	3292	3097
Yorkshire & Humberside	4635	4794	4854
North-West England	6567	6726	6406
East Midlands	3100	3386	3807
West Midlands	4758	5105	5136
East Anglia	1470	1666	1865
South-East England	16271	17133	16729
South-West England	3411	3768	4326
Wales	2644	2724	2790
Scotland	5179	5228	5153
Northern Ireland	1427	1525	1547

Source: Britain, an official handbook

The Planned Location of Industry

The traditional staple industries sited principally in the north of England have declined throughout the Twentieth Century. Successive governments since the 1930's have tried to improve economic conditions in these areas in the following ways:

- Financial incentives: a number of schemes offering financial incentives to firms which re-locate to depressed areas have been implemented since the Special Areas Act of 1934. The Industry Act of 1972 identified three types of areas which qualified for special assistance; these were Special Development Areas (SDA), Development Areas (DA), and Intermediate Areas (IA). During the 1980's the Conservative government progressively reduced both the money available for regional assistance, and the number of areas to which such assistance was given. The government turned its main focus of assistance away from regional aid and concentrated instead upon the provision of aid to 'enterprise zones' in inner city areas. Firms establishing themselves in such zones could obtain the following benefits:

  - 100% capital allowances on commercial and industrial property

  - No liability for development land tax
  - No liability for rates
  - Fewer planning regulations and controls
- Intervention: the government can place orders with firms in development areas, or encourage nationalised industries to do so. It can also bring new towns into existence, by Acts similar to the New Towns Act 1946 and the Town Development Act 1952.
- Legislation: the government can pass legislation which forbids or encourages firms to locate in specific areas.
- Persuasion: the government can encourage firms to relocate to development areas through advertising and the dissemination of information.

Summary

1) The main forms of business organisation are; the sole proprietor, the partnership, limited companies, co-operative retail societies and public enterprises.

2) Internal economies of scale result from the expansion of a single firm: external economies of scale result from the expansion of an entire industry. Firms cannot expand infinitely because demand may be limited, because of the difficulties of raising capital, and because of the Law of Diminishing Returns.

3) The most important influences on the location of industry are: land, power, proximity to raw materials, labour and markets.

4) The main advantages of the localisation of industry are: supply of skilled labour, regional division of labour, development of subsidiary industries and organised markets.

5) The four ways in which government can influence the localisation of industry are: financial incentives, direct intervention, legislation and persuasion.

Self-Assessment Test Three – Questions

1) What are the two main advantages of public enterprises?

2) Give five examples of internal economies of scale.

3) Give three examples of external economies of scale.

4) What are the five most important influences on the location of industry?

5) What are the four main advantages of the localisation of industry?

Self-Assessment Test Three – Answers

1) a) central planning

b) concentration on social objectives instead of the maximisation of profits.

2) a) economies in the use of factors of production

b) economies in administration

c) economies in marketing

d) economies in finance

e) economies in research and development

3) a) supply of skilled labour

b) regional division of labour

c) provision of common services

4) a) land

b) power

c) labour

d) raw materials

e) markets

5) a) creation of a reservoir of skilled labour

b) regional division of labour

c) development of subsidiary industries

d) organised markets

Past Examination Questions on These Topics

1) 'Large firms are always more efficient than small firms'. Examine this statement.

2) 'Regional policy is necessary because of the failure of a freely operating price system to allocate resources efficiently.'

3) In view of the advantages claimed for large-scale production, why do so many small firms continue to flourish?

4) What main factors would influence a firm in choosing the location of a new factory?

5) When a firm increases the extent of its operations it may do so to enjoy economies of scale. What sort of economies are possible and how would they benefit the firm?

4

Market Structures

Objectives

After reading this chapter, you should be able to:

- Distinguish between fixed costs and variable costs
- Distinguish between average cost and marginal cost
- Explain how a monopolist influences the price at which its products are sold
- List the four conditions necessary for price discrimination
- Distinguish between perfect oligopoly and imperfect oligopoly
- List the ways in which monopoly is regulated by governments

Market Structures

Supply under Perfect Competition

Perfect Competition

The demand for most products comes from a large number of buyers who have little ability to act in concert so as to influence prices. In the case of supply, however, economists distinguish between the following conditions:

- Perfect Competition – many producers
- Monopoly – one producer
- Imperfect Competition – few producers

In each of these three conditions the basis of supply is different, as is the ability of a single producer or small number of producers to influence price levels. Supply will be considered first under conditions of perfect competition.

Costs

The term 'cost of production' only has meaning when it is related to output, as the cost of production changes with changes in the level of output. The cost of production of the first motor-car off a production-line might be very high, whilst the cost of the second will be lower, and so on. It is always best to use the term cost of production only when the level of output is stated.

It is important to distinguish between the following kinds of costs:

- Fixed costs: these do not vary over a considerable range of output, and include the cost of buildings, machinery, rent, interest on loans, rates and administration.
- Variable costs: these do vary with changes in the level of output, and include the costs of raw materials, power and labour.
  Some analysts include administrative costs as part of variable costs on the grounds that if demand falls for a considerable period, and workers are either laid off or made redundant, the

costs of administration will be reduced. According to this classification of costs, variable costs are called prime costs, and fixed costs are called supplementary costs. If this latter clarification is accepted, it becomes possible for a firm to survive a falling-of in demand in the short-term if it can meet its prime costs.

– Average and marginal costs: average cost is the average cost of producing each unit of production. Marginal cost is the addition to total cost of each successive unit of production. In the table below, average and marginal costs are given for an imaginary firm.

Output	**Fixed cost**	**Variable cost**	**Total cost**	**Average cost**	**Marginal cost**
50	20	40	60	1.2	–
51	20	82	102	2.0	42
52	20	110	130	2.5	28

As can be seen, total cost (TC) is calculated by adding fixed costs (FC) and variable costs (VC): marginal cost (MC) is the change to total cost of adding one more unit of production.

The next table shows that if average cost is falling, marginal cost will be less than average cost. If average cost is rising, however, marginal cost will be greater than average cost. Average and marginal costs are equal when average cost is at a minimum.

Output	**Total cost**	**Average cost**	**Marginal cost**
20	270	13.5	–
30	330	11.0	6
40	400	10.0	7
50	500	10.0	10
60	630	10.5	13

Output

In economics the term 'normal profit' means the payment necessary to keep an entrepreneur in a particular business, after other costs have been met. An industry expands or contracts according to the ability of firms within it to earn more or less than normal profit. Profit above normal is called 'surplus profit' or 'net revenue'. Economists assume that producers always aim to maximise their profits. The assumption that producers will always act to maximise profits is necessary to a theory of the firm.

A firm's profit is at a maximum when marginal cost is equal to marginal revenue. Marginal revenue is the additional revenue coming into a firm from each additional unit of production. In conditions of perfect competition the price of the product is fixed, so that marginal revenue must be equal to the price of one unit of the commodity. If marginal revenue is greater than marginal cost a firm can expand its output because each additional unit of production will add to its profit. If output is expanded beyond this point, however, marginal cost will be greater than marginal revenue, and total profit will be less. A firm's level of output will be most profitable, therefore, when its marginal cost and marginal revenue are equal. In perfect competition the following relationship holds good:

Price = Marginal cost = Marginal revenue =
Average revenue = Average cost

A firm reaches equilibrium under perfect competition at the level of output where the above relationship is reached: any change in output or method of production will reduce its total profit. An industry is in equilibrium when there is no tendency for the size of the industry to change: firms neither wish to join the industry or leave it.

Monopoly

It will be remembered that a perfect market has six characteristics: homogeneity of product or service, large number of buyers and sellers, buyers and sellers inclose contact, no preferential treatment, free movement into and out of the market, and easily transferable product or service.

Where a monopoly exists, there is only one supplier of a product or service, so that the relationship between supply and demand is very different from that occurring in conditions of perfect competition. There are four major reasons why a monopoly may come into existence:

- A firm may gain control of all the necessary resources for production, allowing it to develop a monopoly. Secondly, a firm may have exclusive control over a product or service by virtue of some technological process not available to potential competitors.

- Legal monopoly: sometimes a company's monopoly is granted it by law, as in the case of the Post Office in Britain.
- Monopoly by collusion: if several producers combine together they can sometimes form an effective monopoly by dominating the market.
- Natural monopoly: this comes about when economies of scale are so important that one firm can produce the total output of an industry at lower cost than would be possible for two or more firms.

Demand and Monopoly

A firm operating in conditions of perfect competition must accept the market price of its product and service as given. A farmer could not ask for more than the market price for his beef, for example, because buyers would refuse to purchase at the higher price. The farmer has no market power, because he cannot influence the price of his product.

For a monopolist, however, the situation is quite different. Such a firm can influence the price at which its products are sold, by increasing or decreasing supply. The monopolist, then, has market power, as the graph below illustrates:

The graph shows that the monopolist influences prices by moving along the demand curve. At point A, for example, the price

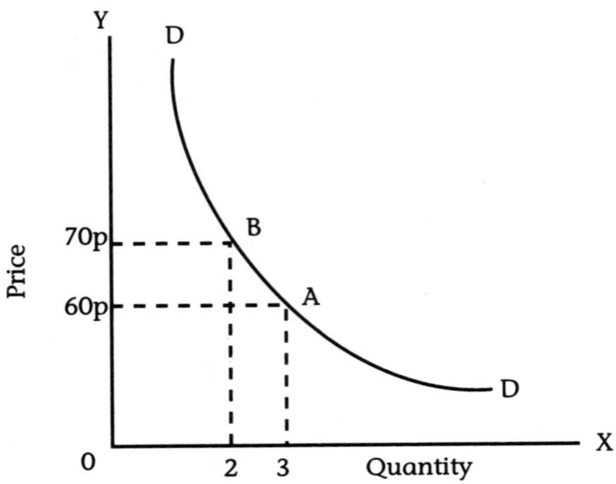

per unit is 60P and the quantity demanded 3: if the monopolist wishes to influence price by reducing the number of units for sale to 2, the demand curve shows that these two units can be sold for >OP (point B). The monopolist can influence price at will by moving along the demand curve in this way: thus a monopolist is a 'price maker', where the product in perfect competition is a 'price taker'.

Price Selection

Any firm maximises profit by selecting an output where marginal cost (MC) equals marginal revenue (MR). It should be noted that where MR = Price for the firm in perfect competition, MR does not equal price for the monopolist. MR is always less than price for the monopolist, as the table below illustrates.

Units Q	**Price Average Revenue**	**Total Revenue (P x Q)**	**Marginal Revenue (MR)**
1	50	50	
2	45	90	90 – 50 = 40
3	40	120	120 – 90 = 30
4	35	140	140 – 120 = 20
5	30	150	150 – 140 = 10
6	25	150	150 – 150 = 0

The monopolist maximises profit by equating MC with MR, as in the graph below:

The monopoly selects Q1 as the output that maximises profits. Any other output, whether greater or smaller, will reduce profit. The maximum price the monopolist can charge for Q1, is determined by

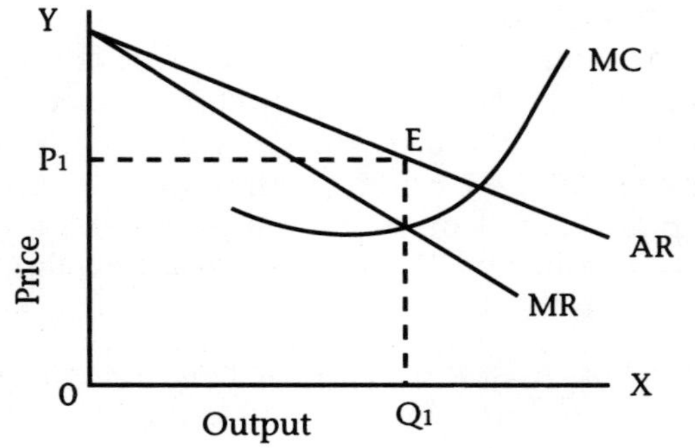

the demand curve: at point E the monopolist can sell Q1, at the price P1.

Price Discrimination

Price discrimination occurs when different consumers are charged different prices for a similar product or service. Price discrimination is made possible under the following conditions:

- a monopoly is the producer
- consumers belong to separate markets
- there is a different elasticity of demand between markets
- the cost of separating markets is not too great

A monopolist can increase his total surplus profit if he sells his monopoly output in one market and a further amount in a second market. This can only be managed successfully if the two markets have different elasticities of demand, otherwise he cannot charge different prices for the product. The price will be higher and the quantity less in the market where demand is more inelastic. Price discrimination is sometimes made possible by separating markets through trade tariffs. A monopoly is maintained in the home market, for example, by import tariffs which keep out foreign goods. Extra output is then sold abroad at a much cheaper price than is obtained in the home market. This practice, known as dumping, sometimes causes producers to complain that foreign competitors are dumping goods at prices below the cost of production. This complaint usually means that the foreign manufacturer is selling the goods below the average cost of production in either market, but above the marginal cost of selling in separate markets.

Other examples of discriminatory pricing include variable railway freight rates, where the fee for carrying expensive commodities is greater than the fee for carrying cheap commodities. This is made possible because different commodities are treated as separate markets. In the case of discriminatory passenger fares the issue of cheap day tickets or period returns creates a second market which attracts a different clientele to that travelling on ordinary tickets. Other examples of price discrimination include:

- geographical price discrimination: where different prices are charged for the same product or service in different areas.

- branding: where a product packaged in two different ways is sold at different prices.
- time: where the price of a product varies over time, as in 'off-peak' electricity.

Supply Under Imperfect Competition

Imperfect competition takes too many forms for all but the few well-defined types to be noted below:

- Monopolistic competition occurs where there are a large number of producers but the product or service is not homogenous.
- Duopoly occurs where there are only two producers or sellers of a product or service.
- Oligopoly occurs where there are only a few producers or sellers of a product or service. Perfect oligopoly occurs where the product or service is homogenous; imperfect oligopoly occurs where there is some differentiation in the product or service.

Monopolistic Competition and the Retail Trade

The retail trade in Britain provides a good example of monopolistic competition, where there are many producers and sellers, but the products are not homogenous. Differentiation in the retail trade occurs even when the product itself is homogenous, because of differences in the quality of service offered, or in the convenience of location of the retail outlet.

One of the most significant effects of monopolistic competition in the retail trade is that it tends to produce excess capacity rather than surplus profit. This is because:

- High-cost firms are able to survive, which they would not be able to do in conditions of perfect competition.
- Many small shops are family businesses, and thus wages are low or effectively subsidised by the owner of the business.
- The smallest retail businesses are carried on by individuals whose major occupation may be unconnected with the retail trade.

It has sometimes been suggested that local authorities should control the tendency towards excess capacity in the retail trade by licensing retail outlets, and this is done in certain cases, local limits being put on the number of fish and chip shops, for example. Wholesalers sometimes act to reduce excess capacity by limiting the number of retailers they will supply in a given area.

Monopolistic Associations

Firms sometimes combine in order to benefit from the advantages of monopoly. In addition to vertical and horizontal integration, the following kinds of association produce monopolistic advantage.

- Voluntary Associations: these work by agreement on a minimum price or restricted output. Note that agreements between firms not to sell below a minimum price were made illegal by the Restrictive Trade Practices Act 1956.
- Cartel: a cartel is a group of independent firms who have agreed to limit output of their product, in order to raise prices. A cartel is usually broken by the action of producers outside it, who increase their own output at the expense of cartel members. A cartel can be established by the government: examples of government established cartels are the British Marketing Boards for potatoes, milk and eggs. The international airlines belong to a cartel called the International Air Transport Association which acts to regulate and standardise passenger air fares.
- Holding company: where a cartel can be broken by one member acting outside the agreement made, a holding company acquires control of member firms by holding a controlling interest in the shares of member firms.
- State monopolies: nationalisation policies in Britain after the Second World War created a number of state monopolies, but there has been a tendency since 1980 for state monopolies to be restored to the private sector, under the 'privatisation' programme of the Conservative government.

Assessment of Monopoly and Imperfect Competition

The main advantages of monopoly are:

- Competition in some industries is wasteful and inefficient, as in the case of gas, electricity and water.

- Excess supply can be eliminated by closing down production centres where costs are high.
- Product differentiation can be limited, as happens in the car industry, where the proliferation of models would increase average costs.

The main disadvantages of monopoly are:

- Prices are higher and output less than under perfect competition.
- Consumer choice is limited under this kind of competition.
- Monopoly firms do not have the same incentive to become efficient as firms operating under perfect competition.

Control of Monopoly

Government action to control monopoly can take the following forms:

- Legal restriction: government limits on profit are one mechanism used to restrict the power of monopolies over consumers.
- State or municipal control: some monopolies have been directly controlled and operated by the state, in order to avoid consumer exploitation.
- In Britain the Monopolies and Restrictive Practices Act 1948 established a Monopolies Commission to examine the conditions of manufacture of a number of commodities. The Monopolies and Mergers Act 1965 gave the Board of Trade the power to examine any proposed merger and refer it to the Monopolies Commission. The Competition Act 1979 extended the powers of the Office of Fair Trading and the Monopolies and Mergers Commission. The Office of Fair Trading can investigate any business activity that it considers likely to reduce competition.

Summary

1) The term 'cost of production' only has meaning when related to output. Fixed costs are those which do not vary over a considerable range of production: variable costs do vary with the level of output. Average cost is the average cost of producing each unit of output.

2) A monopoly exists when there is only one supplier of a product or service. A monopolist seeks to influence price by increasing or decreasing supply.

3) A perfect oligopoly exists where there is a limited number of producers of a homogeneous product. An imperfect oligopoly exists where there is a limited number of suppliers of a product that is differentiated.

4) Government action to regulate monopoly takes three main forms: legal restriction, state or municipal control, and legislation.

Self-Assessment Test Four – Questions

1) Define:
   a) fixed costs
   b) variable costs
   c) average cost
   d) marginal cost

2) How does a monopolist influence the price at which its products are sold?

3) What are the four conditions necessary for price discrimination?

4) Define:
   a) perfect oligopoly
   b) imperfect oligopoly

5) In what three ways is monopoly regulated by government action?

Self-Assessment Test Four-Answers

1) a) costs which do not vary over a considerable range of output.

b) costs which do vary with output.

c) average cost of producing each unit of production

d) addition to total cost of producing each successive unit of production.

2) By increasing or decreasing supply.

3) a) a monopoly is the producer

b) consumers belong to separate markets

c) there is a different elasticity of demand between the markets

d) the cost of separating markets is not too great

4) a) a limited number of producers of a homogenous product

b) a limited number of producers of a product that is differentiated

5) a) legal restriction

b) state or municipal control

c) legislation

Past Examination Questions on These Topics

1) Critically examine the case for and against monopoly, and comment on the policy implications.

2) Compare and contrast the determination of price, output, and profit in an industry under perfect competition and monopoly.

3) In what circumstances may it be desirable to control monopolistic practices, and how might this be done?

4) Why do governments seek to control restrictive practices and monopoly?

5) Explain precisely the difference between fixed and variable costs.

6) What are the arguments for and against the nationalisation of industry? When do you think nationalisation is justified?

5

Market Failure

Objectives

After reading this chapter, you should be able to:

- Distinguish between technical and allocative efficiency
- Describe the characteristics of a public good
- Explain what is meant by positive and negative externalities
- Distinguish between merit goods and demerit goods

Market Failure

Economic Efficiency

Economists use the term 'efficiency' in four different ways when assessing the contribution of different market structures to social welfare. The term carries the following meanings:

- Technical efficiency is achieved when a form of production maximises the output of the available factors of production.
- Productive or cost efficiency is a financial measure of technical efficiency. It is achieved when costs per unit of production are at their lowest.
- X-efficiency is a measure of how closely a firm produces a unit of output at the average total cost curve: X-inefficiency is a measure of how far a firm's costs are in excess of this amount.
- Allocative efficiency is a measure of efficiency of all the industries and markets in an economy: it occurs when prices are equal to marginal cost.

Market Failure and Perfect Competition

Even in conditions of perfect competition market failure would be likely to occur as a result of economic inefficiency produced by the following influences:

- If perfect competition produces economies of scale in some firms but not others, because of the limited size of the market, those firms producing without the benefit of economies of scale will be doing so with a measure of productive inefficiency.
- There may not be markets in every product and service that could be produced to satisfy demand. Such markets are known as 'missing markets'.
- Not every market will be in a state of long-run equilibrium at the same time, thus causing a measure of economic inefficiency.

Market Failure and Imperfect Competition

Even those forms of imperfect competition which are not monopolistic result in forms of market failure, particularly where the production of public goods is concerned. A public good may not be produced at all in a free market economy, as Adam Smith recognised when he argued that certain public goods should be produced by the government. Public goods have two characteristics which distinguish them from private goods,

- Non-excludability: public goods are not owned by individuals who exclude others from using or benefiting from them.
- Non-diminishing: most private goods diminish as a result of being used, so that less of them is available for the use of others. Public goods are non-diminishing.

Most public goods are non-pure in the sense that it is possible to restrict the use of them to those who have contributed to their production. The payment of a television licence, for example, theoretically restricts the benefit of public television to those who have paid for it, making public service television an example of a non-pure public good. In Britain public service radio broadcasting is a pure public good because no direct payment is required to use the service. It is therefore non-excluding.

Public goods are non-diminishing because the total benefit available to others is not decreased by the addition of further beneficiaries of them. One more member of the radio audience, for example, does not make less radio available to others. The marginal cost of production of a public good to an additional consumer is zero. In order to ensure allocative efficiency in the production of public goods, therefore, it is necessary that price=marginal cost. The market provision of public goods would require price being greater than marginal cost: it is therefore more efficient to provide public goods through general taxation at no 'price' to the consumer, rather than to provide them through the market.

It is important here to distinguish between public goods and government goods, the latter being defined as any service or product provided by the government. Government goods include public goods such as defence and roads but, they also include a further category of goods called 'merit goods', such as education and health care.

Externalities

An externality is a special category of public good which is received and consumed by a population as a result of the process of production. An externality may be positive or negative, as the examples below explain:

- Externalities of Costs include pollution and other forms of environmental damage resulting from the process of production.
- Externalities of Benefits include positive by-products resulting from the process of production, such as improvements in the transport infra-structure of an industrial town.
- Consumption externalities are the result of an individual or community's consumption, and include utility gains or utility losses passed on to other consumers.
- Production externalities are the result of the process of production.
- Mixed externalities are those which are produced either by the process of production and are passed on to the consumer, or are produced by the consumer and passed on to the producer in terms of benefits and costs.

Externalities received by the producer which reduce the costs of production are examples of external economies: externalities received by the producer which increase the costs of production are examples of external diseconomies.

To qualify as an externality, it is necessary that the reduction or increase of costs or benefits is a by-product of economic activity, and not the result of deliberate economic planning.

The table below illustrates the different types of externality:

	External benefits	**External Costs**
Produced in production and received by production	A small firm benefitting from road transport improvements on an industrial estate due to the arrival of a larger firm	Pollution of farming land due to increased steel production in neighbouring town

Produced in production and received by consumption	Consumer benefit from land drainage scheme undertaken by neighbouring coal industry	Destruction of visual amenities due to open-cast mining.
Produced in consumption and received by consumption	One neighbour benefitting from another's garden as a visual amenity	One neighbour suffering from another's loud music
Produced in consumption and received in production	A commercial photographer benefitting from an increase in visual amenities due to private house restoration	A consumer's contribution to traffic congestion increasing a firm's cost of production

The importance of externalities is that there is a divergence between social costs and benefits and private costs and benefits. When the process of production results in negative production externality, marginal social cost is greater than marginal private cost, but marginal social benefit and marginal private benefit are the same. Marginal external cost is obtained by calculating the difference between marginal social cost and marginal private cost. Therefore:

Marginal Social Cost = Marginal Private Cost + Marginal External Cost

A private firm always seeks to attain that level of output where marginal private benefit equals marginal private cost. The equilibrium for social benefit maximisation is reached when marginal social benefit equals marginal social cost.

To achieve allocative efficiency, there must be no positive or negative externalities, because these make for a difference between marginal private cost and marginal social cost: if price is greater or lesser than marginal social cost, but equal to marginal private cost, there is no equilibrium between price and marginal total cost. In a market economy firms take account only of marginal private cost and marginal private benefit: therefore the existence of externalities results in allocative inefficiency. Externalities result in a difference in real terms between the money cost of production and the total cost of production.

When a process of production results in positive production externality, marginal social cost equals marginal private cost, but marginal social benefit is greater than marginal private benefit. Marginal external benefit is obtained by calculating the difference between marginal social benefit and marginal private benefit. Therefore:

Marginal Social Benefit = Marginal Private Benefit + Marginal External Benefit

A private firm always seeks to attain that level of output where marginal private benefit equals marginal private cost. When there is positive production externality, therefore, there is market failure because there is too little of the product produced and consumed. Positive production externality results in a 'missing' market in the externality.

Public Policy and Positive and Negative Externality

When production externality is produced, the public policy issue is to take suitable action to restore an equilibrium between marginal social benefit and marginal social cost. The following measures are used to achieve this end:

- Regulation and quantity controls are used to ban or inhibit negative production externalities. Regulation and quantity controls can also be used to ensure positive production externalities.
- Taxation and subsidies can also be used to correct market failure resulting from positive or negative externalities.

Market Failure and Equity

So far in this discussion of market failure the main consideration has been given to productive and allocative efficiency. Productive efficiency occurs when average costs are minimised: allocative efficiency occurs when price equals marginal social cost. These kinds of economic efficiency are sometimes called Pareto efficiency, who first developed this concept of economic efficiency.

Pareto efficiency has little to do with the equitable distribution of income and wealth. One of the most significant forms of market failure occurs because of inequitable distributions of wealth and income. Some economists argue that markets should be replaced by a command mechanism which would ensure the equitable distribution of wealth and income: others argue only that markets should be modified to ensure the equitable distribution of wealth and income. In most Western economies taxation is used as the main instrument for modifying the market in order to redistribute wealth and income. Re-distributive taxation policies produce a degree of inefficiency within the market, but the equitable re-distribution of wealth and income is sometimes felt to justify these distortions.

One other area of public policy in which non-economic considerations contribute to manipulation of the market occurs in the case of merit and demerit goods. A merit good is a product or service from which the social benefits of consumption exceed the private benefit to the consumer. A demerit good is a product or service from which the social cost of consumption exceeds the private cost to the consumer.

The market can provide merit goods such as education and health-care, but there will be a tendency for these goods to be under-consumed if supplied at market prices. There is thus a policy problem for governments to increase the consumption of merit goods. This can be done by requiring the consumption of merit goods through legislation, as in the case of compulsory motor insurance. Other merit goods are provided free at the point of use, as in the case of hospital treatment in Britain, which is financed through public taxation.

Demerit goods are provided by the market, but need to be regulated because the marginal social cost of their consumption exceeds their marginal private cost. Alcohol is an example of a demerit good. Taxation is used to regulate the supply of demerit goods through price manipulation; in the case of some demerit goods, such as certain kinds of fire-arm or dangerous drugs, the criminal law in Britain bans the demerit good altogether.

Summary

1) Technical efficiency consists of the maxamisation of output of the available factors of production. Allocative efficiency is a measure of the efficiency of all the markets in an economy; it occurs when price equals marginal cost.

2) The two chief characteristics of a public good are non-exludability and non-diminishability.

3) Positive and negative externalities produce a divergence between social costs and benefits and private costs and benefits.

Self-Assessment Test Five – Questions

1) Define:
a) technical efficiency

b) allocative efficiency

2) What are the two chief characteristics of a public good?

3) What is the main economic significance of positive and negative externalities?

4) What is one of the principal ways in which governments seek to re-distribute wealth and income equitably?

Self-Assessment Test Five – Answers

1) a) maximisation of output of the available factors of production.

b) measure of efficiency of all the industries and markets in an economy: occurs when price equals marginal cost.

2) a) non-excludability

b) non-diminishability

3) they create a divergence between social costs and benefits and private costs and benefits.

4) taxation.

Past Examination Questions on These Topics

1) Suggest the main deficiencies of an economy which is regulated solely by a laissez-faire price system.
2) Outline four possible ways in which taxation can be used as an instrument of economic policy.
3) 'Economics is concerned with the problem of allocation'. Discuss.
4) Using economic theory, explain why a government may have to intervene in the operation of the price system to improve the allocation of resources.
5) Explain, with examples, the main sources of 'market failure' in a free market economy.

6

The Distribution of the National Income

Objectives

After reading this chapter, you should be able to:

- List the three ways in which national income can be calculated
- List the three main influences on the elasticity of demand for the factors of production
- List the five major influences liable to produce business uncertainty

The Distribution of the National Income

The National Income

A country achieves a certain output of products and services each year as a result of its employment of the factors of production. The total volume of production achieved in a given year is the country's total income. Although each of the factors of production may be seen as earning its own kind of payment, it is difficult in certain circumstances to identify factor payments. Labour, for example, obviously earns wages, but it cannot be said that rent is paid exclusively for the use of land; neither can the payment of interest for the use of capital always be made distinct from profit, which is payment for the services of the entrepreneur.

The entrepreneur regards payments to the other factors of production as part of the total costs of production, while these same payments are regarded by the persons receiving them as income. It is important to note that payments are always made to persons for the use of inanimate factors, and not to the factors themselves. Thus rent is paid to the owner of land, and interest to the owner of capital. Income, therefore, has two sources:

- performance of personal service.
- ownership of inanimate factors of production.

Inequality of income results from differences in the level of payments for personal service, and from differences in the amount of property possessed. Property includes land, buildings, shares in companies, and any form of capital.

In countries where taxation is intended to reduce the inequality of income between individuals, it is usual to tax income progressively, and to tax property above a specified minimum amount.

The national income is equivalent to the volume of production because the amount paid for a product is really a series of payments for all the services undertaken in its production, these payments constituting the income of those receiving them. The national income is therefore equal to the total income of all individuals over a given year, or the money value of all the products and services produced in a given year. It is usual to estimate the national income in terms of money value because this is easier to determine than the amount of some services provided, such as medicine or education. Another method of calculating national income is by estimating total consumption for a given year: as income is either spent or saved, the totals of both amounts added together will also be equal to national income.

National Income = Volume of Production = Total Consumption + Total Savings.

Calculation of the National Income

In Britain the government issues a White Paper in March every year which provides details of the national income for the previous year. The total value of all the goods and services produced in a year is known as the Gross Domestic Product: this is calculated at factor cost, without taking into account the effect of government subsidies or taxation.

When the value of exports less the value of imports has been added to Gross Domestic Product the resulting sum is known as Gross National Product at Factor Cost. National Income is obtained by subtracting capital consumption (amount spent on making up for the depreciation of capital equipment), from the Gross National Product.

National Income = Gross National Product at Factor Cost + Net Value of Exports less the Value of Imports – Capital Consumption.

A second method of calculating national income is to add together all the incomes derived from production, making allowance for incomes derived from capital consumption.

National Income = Total Incomes from Production – Incomes derived from Capital Consumption.

A third method of calculating national income is to add together all expenditure, including public authority expenditure, again making allowance for capital consumption.

National Income =Total Personal Expenditure + Public Authority Expenditure – Capital Consumption.

A number of influences affect the size of a country's income, chief amongst which are:

- The stock of factors of production: this is one of the most important influences on a country's national income. The stock of land varies from one country to another, as does climate, which determines both the nature and extent of agricultural production. The stock of labour is dependent on the country's population level, and the quality and extent of education and training. The stock of capital also varies, from primitive tools to modern industrial plant.
- Technical knowledge: this is the second major influence on a country's national income, and has important implications both for a country's total volume of production, and the degree of specialization within the economy.
- Politics: this is the third major influence on a country's national income. Political stability encourages both domestic and foreign investment, whereas political instability inhibits investment.

Although calculation of the national income is theoretically straightforward, there are a number of practical difficulties of which the economist needs to be aware. The most important of these are:

- Inadequate information: Income tax returns are never a completely reliable indication of a country's economic activity, because some work is always excluded from them.
- Double counting: The cost of raw materials and of finished goods must not both be counted, as the cost of raw materials would then be counted twice. All services performed by one firm for another must be deducted from the second firm's output.
- Unpaid services: Only those services for which payment is made may be counted as part of the national income. Unpaid work or favours for friends are therefore excluded from the calculation of national income. The result is the anomaly that national income can be increased without being accompanied by an increase in the volume of production, if people who have previously cleaned their own houses, for example, take to paying others to perform this service.
- Depreciation: If the net national income is to be calculated, some allowance for the cost of replacing obsolete fixed capital assets must be made.

- Housing: A portion of rent paid for housing must be allowed for depreciation of the asset, when the landlord's income is calculated. In the case of an owner-occupier it is usual to consider that his house produces a 'notional' income equal to its rentable value.
- Public income and expenditure: Government spending is of three major kinds, defence and the maintenance of internal law and order, the provision of social services, and the payment of interest on the national debt. Government income is derived principally from national taxation, and local authority income from rates on business property: note that since April 1990 domestic rates in England have been replaced by the Community Charge. It is usual to regard most government spending as a payment made by the taxpayer for services, although payment of interest on the national debt and social welfare payments are not included in calculations of national income because they are transfers of personal income and may not be counted twice.
- Foreign payments: It is usual to include total receipts less payments when calculating the effect of foreign payments on the national income.
- Changes in money value: Measurement of the national income in money terms has little meaning unless comparisons between different years are calculated in terms of prices ruling in a selected base year.

The National Income and Economic Growth.

Calculations of the national income are important to economists because they reveal the annual volume of production of a country. A country's economic welfare is partly dependent on the total volume of production, and partly on the way income is distributed. A country may have a large volume of production, but living standards will be low if there is great inequality of income between the poorer classes and the richer ones.

The rate of increase of a country's national income is a good indicator of that country's rate of economic growth, and usually of the standard of living. When calculations of national income are used to compare living standards over a certain period or between different countries, account must be taken of the following:

- Price changes.
- Population increase or decrease in the period or countries studied.
- Exchange rate between the countries studied.
- Percentage of production concentrating on armaments.
- The amount of unpaid work individuals perform for themselves, which is liable to be very high in third-world countries.
- The inequality of income.

The Distribution of the National Income.

Supply and Demand for the Factors of Production.

The demand for the factors of production is a 'derived' demand, because it depends ultimately on the demand for the products and services for the production of which the factors are necessary. In modern economies production is carried on in anticipation of the future demand for products and services: this being so, the demand for factors is also based on the anticipation of future demand. There are three main influences on the elasticity of demand for the factors of production:

- Elasticity of demand for finished products: The elasticity of demand for factors is a measurement of the responsiveness of demand for factor services to changes in factor prices. Factor demand is elastic when a slight fall in its price increases demand. As the demand for factors is a derived demand, it is dependent on the elasticity of demand for the finished products for which factors are used.
- Factor quantity required: if only a small amount of a factor is required in the production of a product, then demand for that factor will be fairly inelastic.
- Substitution between factors: where one factor can be substituted for another in the production of a product, demand for both factors will be elastic, as producers respond to price rises in one factor by switching to the other. A producer may replace labour with machinery if wages are high, or replace machinery with labour if wages are low.

  The following influences affect the supply of the factors of production:

- Land. Although land is a 'gift of nature', and has no cost of production, its supply cannot be regarded as absolutely fixed, because land can be taken from one use and applied to another, when conditions make the alternative use economical.
- Labour. The supply of labour may increase as a result of increased living standards, as people may then marry younger (causing the gap between generations to close), and live longer. As with land, the supply of labour can be applied to different uses, as a result of changes in wage levels between industries. The cost of production of labour can be calculated in terms of the cost of providing health and education services for the population.
- Capital. The basis of the supply of capital is saving; the supply of capital goods increases as their price increases.

The elasticity of supply for the factors of production is a measurement of the responsiveness of supply of factor services to changes in factor prices. The following should be noted in relation to each of the factors of production:

- Land. The supply of land is usually fairly elastic over a long period, especially in the case of land for agricultural purposes.
- Labour. The supply of labour is determined by occupational specificity and occupational mobility. When occupational specificity is high, supply is fairly inelastic because it takes time to re-train workers. Where geographical mobility is high, and workers can respond to higher wages by re-locating to other areas, supply tends to be elastic.
- The supply of capital also depends on its specificity, although capital is usually responsive to price increases. The supply of some forms of capital, such as machinery, is elastic because more of it can be quickly produced. The supply of other forms of capital, such as mineral deposits, may be fairly inelastic because the supply of it cannot be increased quickly.

Rent

The term 'rent' is used by economists not only in connection with land, but to describe a surplus payment made to any factor of production. The surplus, or economic rent, is that portion of the total payment which exceeds what is necessary to keep a factor in employment. In the case of wages, for example, a man who would be prepared to work for £200 per week, but whose actual wages are £250 per week, receives a surplus, or economic rent of £50 per week. Where a factor has a great degree of specificity, and could not therefore be applied to another form of production, it is possible to regard the major portion of the total payment received for its use as economic rent. 'Transfer earnings' describes the amount a factor could earn in its best-paid alternative employment. Any amount paid in excess of transfer earnings is therefore rent. A second definition of rent is that it is a surplus paid to any factor the supply of which is not easily increased, and that it results from increased demand for that factor.

It is possible to establish whether the extra payment to a factor is rent by determining whether the extra payment is the result of an increase in the price of the product or service. Rent is always the result of an increase in the price of the product or service.

Theories of Wages

Economists do not distinguish between wages and salaries except when discussing costs, when wages are regarded as varying with output but salaries, at least in the short-term, are regarded as fixed. A distinction is made, however, between real and nominal wages. Nominal or money wages are wages paid in money, and real wages are a measure of the amount of products or services which can be bought. In times of inflation it is possible for money wages to rise whilst real wages are falling or remaining constant. A further distinction is made between wage rates and earnings: earnings frequently outstrip wage rates, as people work over-time.

Three main theories of wages will now be considered: the marginal productivity theory, the market theory, and the wage bargaining theory.

The marginal theory of distribution argues that the maximum a producer will pay for any factor of production is the value of its marginal product, since to pay more would be to increase costs in excess of revenue. This theory is the basis for the marginal productivity theory of wages. The theory has been criticized on the following grounds:

- it is impossible to calculate the value of the marginal product of any factor of production.

- the efficiency of labour depends on the quality of the other factors of production employed.
- a small increase or decrease in wages may not alter the amount of labour employed by an entrepreneur, who may be influenced more by his estimate of future demand.
- the theory is only applicable under conditions of perfect competition, and so has little relevance to actual conditions.

The market theory of wages regards them as the price paid to labour for its services. Wages, it is argued, are subject to the same laws of demand and supply as other products and services. It is difficult to regard the labour market as similar to the markets for other products and services, however, because of the difficulty of assessing the cost of production of labour, except where a specific form of training needs to be undergone. The demand for labour, as has been seen, is a derived demand, based on the producer's anticipation of demand for his product or service. Although it is generally the case that an increase in price will result in an increase in the supply of labour, it sometimes happens that increased wages result in a reduced supply of labour, as individuals spend more time on leisure activities, rather than working as many hours as before.

Some economists believe that the determination of wages by collective bargaining creates conditions of imperfect competition for wages, and that a theory of wages should take account of this. Collective bargaining results in bi-lateral monopoly, the trade union being the monopolist supplier, and the employer's association being the monopolist buyer of labour. Proponents of the bargaining theory of wages argue that wage levels depend on the bargaining strength of trade unions: differences in wage levels between industries are interpreted as differences in the relative strengths of the trade unions involved. It has to be said, however, that a trade union's strength depends on the size of its membership, the nature of the industry whose members it represents, and general economic conditions: it is easier for all trade unions to bargain in periods of high employment than in periods of high unemployment. The marginal productivity theorists argue that trade unions can negotiate money wages that are higher than the marginal product of labour during inflationary times: but that real wages can only be increased as the result of an increase in the volume of production.

Wages Systems

The most usual method of payment for labour is the standard rate, which frees both the employer and employee from having to negotiate an individual rate, and allows the employer to calculate his labour costs exactly. Standard rates are also essential to collective bargaining.

Piece-rates are a wages system based on the amount of work carried out by an employee, rather than on his hours of attendance at work. Piece-rates can only be operated where an individual or small group's output is easily quantifiable. The main advantages of the piece-rate system are;

- it acts as an incentive and rewards output
- it reduces the need for close supervision of employees
- it keeps calculations of the costs of production simple. Its main disadvantages are;
  - it rewards speed rather than skill, although for some tasks speed and skill are synonymous
  - it can result in the piece-rate being reduced in real terms as employers reduce the wage rate per piece against the time rate.

Several more complex incentives have been developed, among the most important of which are various bonus systems. A premium bonus system calculates how much output should be produced in a given time at a given price. Workers are paid a bonus if they produce more output in the given time: the bonus is calculated on the basis of the time saved. The task-bonus scheme works by paying a bonus if a task is performed within a specified time: in some variants of the scheme the bonus payments vary according to how closely the worker's finishing time approaches the agreed period.

Interest and Profit

Income is payment for services rendered to production, and is paid either in return for personal services or for the impersonal services provided by the owner of property. Wages are payment for labour. As has been seen, it is difficult to assign rent to particular factors of production. Interest is payment received for the use of capital, and profit is payment to the entrepreneur for his services. Alternatively, interest can be seen as income from money capital, and profit as income from real capital.

In a modern economy the principal lenders of money are:

- Banks, which lend to the government through the purchase of Government securities, and to businesses and individuals.
- Building societies, which lend money for the purchase of houses and business property.
- Finance and credit companies which lend to individuals for the purchase of consumer items.
- Insurance companies, which lend to the government through the purchase of Government securities, and to businesses through the purchase of company debentures.
- Businesses, which lend to the government through the purchase of Government securities, and to banks and financial institutions through deposits.
- Individuals, who lend to the Government through the purchase of Government securities, to businesses through the purchase of shares and debentures, and to banks, building societies and finance companies through personal deposits.

The principal borrowers in a modern economy are:

- the government.
- banks and building societies.
- businesses.

The gross interest on any loan is made up of three elements. The first of these is a payment for risk, so that a large company will pay a lower rate of interest on a loan from its bank than will a sole trader or individual. Similarly, an unsecured loan will attract a higher rate of interest than a loan secured on property or some other form of capital. A charge is also added to interest for the work involved in setting up a loan, the banks calling this addition to interest a facilitation charge. The third element in gross interest is pure or net interest. Where the elements charged for risk and for the work involved in setting up the loan will vary from one borrower to another, pure or net interest remains the same for all but the very largest borrowers.

A government borrows money by offering bonds for sale which bear an attractive rate of interest over the period of the loan. A government may thus issue 10% National bonds redeemable 1995-2000, the dates specifying that the bonds will become payable between the two dates. £1,000 worth of these bonds will therefore bring an income of £100 per year. Such bonds can be traded on the stock exchange, where their value fluctuates daily. If a new government issue offers bonds at 15% interest, perhaps to make the investment attractive in a period of inflation, the demand for the initial issue of 10% bonds will decline, and their market price will fall: in this case the market price for the £1,000 worth will become about £700, so that the rate of yield on this issue to the new purchaser will be comparable to the rate of yield on the new issue.

Saving

Loans occur because the borrower wishes to gain access to products or services, and calculates that the value of his satisfaction from so doing will be at least equal to the value of the sum borrowed and the interest payable on the sum borrowed. For borrowing to take place, there must be savings which can be lent. Savings occur when consumption is foregone, so that any reduction in consumption can be regarded as saving. It is important to realize that saving makes real investment possible, the accumulation of capital goods that will increase the volume of production. The following are the main kinds of saving:

- Corporate saving is the undistributed profits of limited companies.
- Individual saving is the amount of money held or invested by individuals.
- Compulsory saving occurs through taxation which limits consumption and so makes real investment possible.
- Forced saving occurs in periods of inflation when real incomes do not rise. This inhibits consumption and so makes real investment possible.

Although it is generally true that savings are a reflection of interest rates, there are other factors which influence the extent of saving, the most important of which are:

- Saving for future needs or contingency saving. Individual savings are usually intended to make specific purchases possible, or to be a form of insurance against unfavourable personal circumstances.
- Unplanned saving. Individuals in the highest income brackets frequently save large amounts after meeting their personal needs.

The Rate of Interest

There are many theories about what determines the rate of interest in an economy. The supply and demand theorists argue that the interest on loans is equivalent to their price, and that their price is determined by the demand for loans and the available supply of them. The natural rate of interest is seen as the rate at which demand and supply are equal. Time-preference theorists, on the other hand, argue that most people prefer to have money in the present than in the future, so that the supply of loans depends on the interest rate being sufficiently attractive to persuade people to forego current consumption. The liquidity-preference view of interest argues that the rate of interest is not determined solely by the demand for loans and the supply of savings. Supporters of this view point to the fact that banks are able to create credit, and that individuals like to hold money balances, neither of which would occur if the interest rate was determined solely by demand and supply. Proponents of the liquidity-preference theory argue that savings will be low when the price of securities is expected to rise, as people will use their money balance to buy: savings will be high when the price of securities is expected to fall, as people will refrain from buying. Liquidity theorists argue that the rate of interest should be seen as the reward for parting with liquidity.

Profit

It is important to distinguish between gross profit, net profit and pure profit. Gross profit is the total revenue of a company before its costs have been taken into account. Net profit is obtained by subtracting costs from gross profit.

A third element in profit is pure profit. Some economists define pure profit as the reward of the entrepreneur for his share in the work production. Others see pure profit as a surplus remaining after all the costs of production, including the wages of management, have been met. Whatever view is taken, pure profit goes to the owner of a business, and is a reward for risk-bearing. It is important to realize that the entrepreneur's income is residual, unlike the other costs of production, and can therefore be negative. All businesses carry a degree of risk or uncertainty, because production is based on anticipated demand; in a situation where there was no risk, there could be no pure profit. The following are the major influences liable to result in uncertainty:

- changes in demand due to changes in the level of population or its age distribution.
- changes in demand due to changes in fashion.
- changes in demand due to changes in total income or changes in the way income is distributed.
- changes in technology which alter methods of production.
- lack of knowledge of rival firms' price and output policies.

As has been stated elsewhere, normal profit is the payment necessary to keep an entrepreneur in a specific line of production, and can therefore be regarded as part of the cost of production. Pure profit, however, is an additional payment made to the entrepreneur for his skill: it is therefore part of his earned income, and should not be regarded as a cost of production. High profits, therefore, do not cause high prices, but are the result of high prices, which themselves are caused by a high level of demand.

Summary

1) National Income can be calculated in any of the following three ways. NI=GDP at factor cost + Net Value of Exports less the Value of Exports – Capital Consumption: NI = Total Incomes from Production – Incomes derived from Capital Consumption: NI = Total Personal Expenditure + Public Authority Expenditure – Capital Consumption.

2) The three main influences on the elasticity of demand for the factors of production are: elasticity of demand for finished products, factor quantity required, and substitution between factors.

3) The three main theories of wages are: marginal productivity theory, market theory and wage-bargaining theory.

4) The five influences liable to produce business uncertainty are: changes in population level or age-distribution, changes in fashion, changes in total income or income distribution, changes in methods of production, and ignorance of rival firms' output and price policies.

Self-Assessment Test Six – Questions

1) What are the three main influences on the elasticity of demand for the factors of production?

2) What are the three main theories of wages considered in the text?

3) What are the five major influences liable to produce business uncertainty?

Self-Assessment Test Six – Answers

1) a) elasticity of demand for finished products

b) factor quantity required

c) substitution between factors

2) a) marginal productivity theory

b) market theory

c) wage-bargaining theory

3) a) changes in demand due to changes in the level of population or its age distribution

b) changes in demand due to changes in fashion

c) changes in demand due to changes in total income or the distribution of income

d) changes in technology which alter methods of production

e) lack of knowledge of rival firms' price and output policies

Past Examination Questions on These Topics

1) What are the limitations of Gross National Product (GNP) at current prices as a measure of change in the economic welfare of a community? What further information would you require better to assess welfare changes?

2) National Income = National Outlay = National Product. Explain in actual calculations what are the most important adjustments which have to be made to each?

3) Explain two of the following concepts:

a) fixed and variable costs

b) economic rent

c) elasticity of supply

4) Analyse the main purposes of National Income calculations.

5) 'A trade union can only raise the real wages of its members at the expense of reduced employment for its members.' Discuss.

6) Explain the methods used in calculating a country's National Income. For what purposes can such calculations be used?

7) Define the term national income and explain how it can be measured. Does the national income necessarily reflect the standard of living of a country's inhabitants?

7

Investment

Objectives

After reading this chapter, you should be able to:

- Outline the main elements of the discounted cash flow method of investment appraisal
- Outline the main elements of the marginal efficiency of investment theory
- Outline the main elements of the accelerator theory of investment

Investment

Investment and the Single Firm

A firm's demand for the services of a factor of production depends on two variables: the productivity of the factor and the price or cost of using it. The marginal productivity theory can be applied to investment, in which case the theory states that investment will be at the level where marginal revenue productivity (MRP) of capital equals the cost of capital, by which is meant the rate of interest. Substitution between the factors of production allows a firm to change its demand for factors as their relative price changes. A fall in the rate of interest, for example, makes capital relatively cheaper than labour. A firm may thus decide to increase its borrowing in order to adopt more capital-intensive methods of production than were employed when the cost of labour was low relative to the cost of capital.

Although a firm may estimate that an investment in new capital is justified if the marginal productivity of capital equals the rate of interest, the rate of interest is subject to fluctuations over a long period. A firm must take into account the likely returns on an investment in new capital over the economic life of the investment. This estimate is of the expected future productivity of the investment. A firm concerned with the maximisation of profits will decide that investment in a capital asset is worthwhile if the rate of return per period expected over the life of the investment is greater than the expected percentage rate of interest payable on the funds borrowed to finance the investment. When forecasting, the firm cannot be certain of:

- future rates of interest
- net returns produced in each year of the investment's life
- the economic life of the investment, which may be shortened by changes in technology

The Discounted Cash Flow Method of Investment Appraisal

A firm using the discounted cash flow method of investment appraisal proceeds by calculating the asset's expected returns for each year of its life. The firm then subtracts a discount rate to calculate the present value (PV) of future expected income. By this method of appraisal income received in the future is worth less than income received in the present, because of the effect on the value of money of the interest rate. The formula for calculating present value is:

$$PV = \frac{Yn}{(1+r)^n}$$

where:

PV = Present Value
n = Number of years of the investment
Y = Year
r = Current or expected rate of interest, used as a discount rate

In the DCF formula, 'r' is the test rate of discount selected by a company to calculate the present value of a future source of income. The test selected will be either the rate of interest, or the cost of borrowing.

A second measure used by companies is to calculate the internal rate of return of an investment, using the formula:

$$\text{Initial Cost of Investment} = \frac{Yn}{(1 + i)^n}$$

where Yn = number of years of the investment
i = internal rate of return.

For each investment the internal rate of return in that rate of discount which would make the present value of the future source of income equal to the initial cost of the investment.

Macroeconomic Theories of Investment

Marginal Efficiency of Investment Theory

According to the marginal efficiency of investment theory, there exists within an economy a large number of possible investments not yet undertaken, each with its own internal rate of return calculated as shown above. A calculation of the internal rate of return of all these investments would result in a ranking of the investments in descending order of expected future yields. The resulting curve is known as the marginal efficiency of investment function, and is illustrated below:

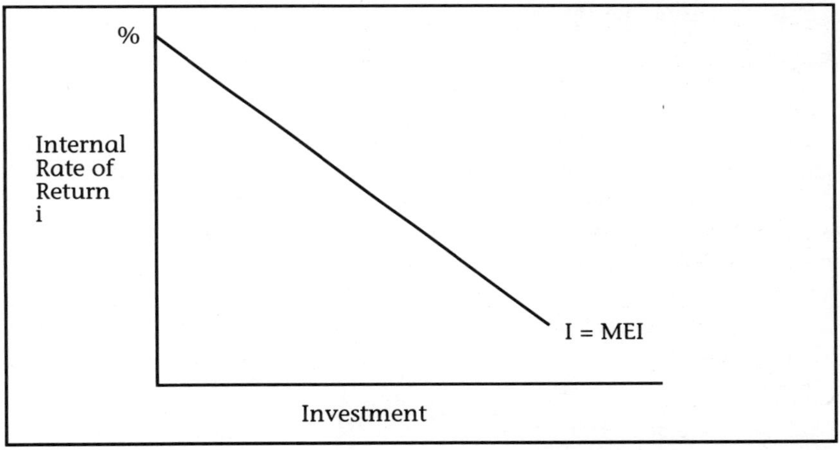

According to this theory, the aggregate level of investment is determined by the prevailing rate of interest on borrowed capital. The equilibrium level of aggregate investment occurs when the marginal efficiency of capital equals the rate of interest.

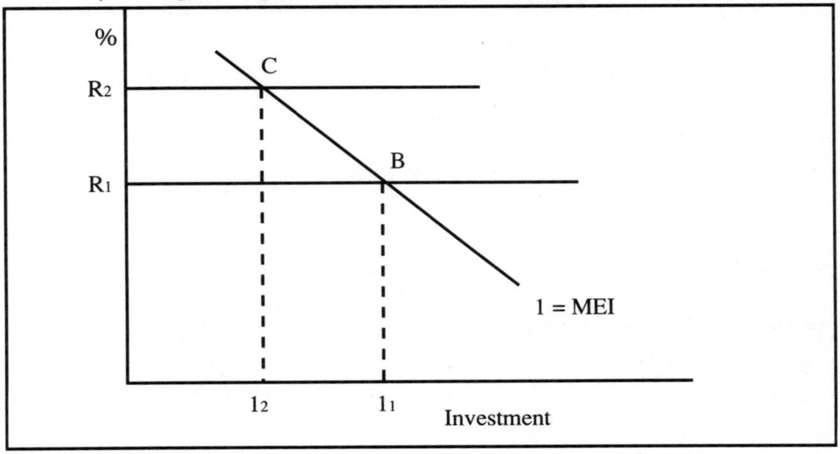

In the graph above the rate of interest is initially R1, and the aggregate demand for investment occurs at B, where investment is I1,: if the interest rate rises to R2, aggregate demand for investment falls to C, where investment is I2.

Keynes argued that the expectations of businessmen cause the position of the MEI curve to change. If firms are optimistic about the future, their estimates of profit and income from investment rise, pushing the MEI curve outwards.

The Accelerator Theory of Investment

Unlike the MEI theory of the aggregate level of investment which is based on the investment decision making process of a single firm, the accelerator theory is based on the assumption that all firms strive to keep a relatively fixed ratio between current output and their present stock of fixed capital assets. This is known as the 'capital output ratio'. A capital output ratio of 4 means that £4.00 of capital is required in order to produce £1.00 of output. In this theory, the level of current net investment in fixed capital assets is dependent on the change in income or output on the previous year. This is expressed in the formula:

$$I_t = v\,(Y_t - Y_{t-1})$$

where:
I_t =Net investment this year
Y_t =Current national income
Y_{t-1} =National income last year
v =Capital output ratio.

In the table below imaginary levels of national income are shown for the years 1990 to 1993. Capital output ratio is 2.

Year	**Current Income in millions**	**Previous Income in millions**	**Investment in millions**
1990	100	90	2 (100–90) = 20
1991	150	100	2 (150–100)= 100
1992	250	150	2 (250–150) = 200
1993	360	250	2 (360–250) = 220

According to the accelerator theory it is the rate of growth of national income which determines investment, rather than growth in itself. The theory states that:

– investment is constant when the rate of growth of annual national income is constant.

- investment increases when the rate of growth of annual national income accelerates.
- investment decreases when the rate of growth of annual national income decelerates.

The accelerator theory has been criticised for its assumption that all firms react in the same way to changes in the demand for their products. It has also been criticised because it leaves out of account spare capacity which can be used instead of investment to respond to short-term increases in demand.

Summary

1) The discounted cash flow method of investment appraisal regards future income as worth less than present income, because of the effects of interest.

2) According to the marginal efficiency of investment theory, the equilibrium level of aggregate investment is reached when the marginal efficiency of capital equals the rate of interest.

3) The main assumption of the accelerator theory of investment is that firms strive to keep a constant ratio between production levels and their stock of fixed capital assets.

Self-Assessment Test Seven – Questions

1) Why does the discounted cash flow method of investment appraisal regard future income as worth less than present income?

2) What is the equilibrium level of aggregate investment, according to the marginal efficiency of investment theory?

3) What is the main assumption of the accelerator theory of investment?

Self-Assessment Test Seven – Answers

1) The value of money declines as a result of the interest rate.

2) Marginal efficiency of capital equals the rate of interest.

3) Firms strive to keep a constant ratio between production levels and their stock of fixed capital assets.

Past Examination Questions on These Topics

1) What are the main factors determining the level of investment in a country? What is the importance of the level of investment to an economy?

2) What are the main determinants of the level of business investment?

3) a) Define:

i) gross investment

ii) depreciation

iii) net investment

b) What are the main factors affecting the level of investment in a country?

4) a) Define 'investment'

b) Consider the view that a high level of investment is essential for sustained economic growth.

8

International Trade and Foreign Exchange

Objectives

After reading this chapter, you should be able to:

- List the geographical factors which influence a country's forms of production
- List the assumptions on which the theory of trade is based
- List the three groups of payments included in a nation's balance of payments
- Understand the relative advantages and disadvantages of fixed and floating exchange rates

International Trade and Foreign Exchange

International Trade

The Theory of Comparative Cost

International trade first began when one country could produce things which other countries desired but were unable to produce for themselves. The reasons why one country may be able to produce something that others cannot may be due to geographical differences:

- Mineral deposits can only be worked in regions where they occur
- Many commodities require special conditions of climate or soil if they are to be grown successfully
- Some countries develop skills in the production of specific commodities such as the growing of grapes for wine

International trade in the contemporary world is not based on one country's inability to be a producer of the articles it desires, as in the past, but on the principle of comparative cost. Britain, for example, imports many commodities which it could produce for itself, such as wheat and dairy produce, but it specialises in the production of other goods instead, by the export of which it is able to finance the import of wheat and dairy produce. International specialisation is an expansion of the division of labour, and has contributed greatly to the increase in world output which has occurred over the last one hundred years.

A nation's choice of the forms of production in which it specialises is determined by its advantages over other countries in the production of certain goods. This is the Principle of Comparative Advantage. A country's decision to specialise in one form of production rather than another is based on whether it can produce the same quantity of a particular good more cheaply than other countries. This is the Principle of Comparative Cost, which is really an extension of the Principle of Comparative Advantage. Comparative cost is calculated by considering the quantity of a good that can be produced by a given quantity of the factors of production.

The expression 'terms of trade' refers to the rate at which one country's products are exchanged for the products of another country. The terms of trade depend on the relative strength of demand for the products involved. The terms of trade are favourable to a country when the prices of its exports are high compared to the prices of its imports.

The theory of international trade is based on a number of assumptions:

- perfect competition between nations
- full employment in all countries
- no restrictions on currency transfers
- no trade restrictions in the form of tariffs or quotas

It should also be borne in mind that the theory of international trade takes no account of the influence on prices of transport costs, or the effects of increasing or diminishing returns.

Protectionism and Free Trade

Every country limits free trade to a greater or lesser extent, either through tariffs which are a tax on imported goods, or through quotas, which limit the amount of goods that can be imported. Tariffs are used to protect a country's industries which would become essential in time of war, and for short-term economic reasons. Protectionism for non-economic reasons takes the following forms:

- Adam Smith in the 'Wealth of Nations' argued that national defence should be undertaken by the government as the market would be unwilling, or unable, to provide national defence. The manufacture of weapons and military technology is a protected industry because of its importance: no country would like to be dependent on imports of weapons or military equipment in time of war, or to export military products to potential enemy states. There is little to be said for free trade in the arms industry.
- In democracies there may be political pressure to maintain tariffs or quotas in order to protect domestic employment in certain industries. During the 1970's trade unionists in Britain argued that 'cheap' imports of coal, iron and steel should be subject to

import control in order to protect British workers from what was described as 'unfair competition' from abroad.

The economic arguments in favour of protectionism are:

- It is sometimes argued that buying goods from abroad weakens the domestic economy by acting as a drain on resources. This argument only holds good when the net value of imports exceeds the net value of exports. In the Nineteenth Century Britain's imports of raw materials from America, Australia and Canada provided those countries with the sterling which they required to buy finished products from Britain.
- It is also argued that tariffs and quotas diversify a country's economic activity, making the production of goods that were previously imported relatively cheaply, economically viable. There is some truth in this argument, although it must be borne in mind that diversification caused by tariffs and quotas results from the creation of an artificial comparative advantage which can only be maintained by restrictions on trade.
- Another argument favouring tariffs and quotas is that newly-established or infant industries may require assistance until they achieve the economies of scale necessary for full competition with the established industries of other countries.
- It is sometimes argued that tariffs and quotas reduce the price of goods, if the country importing the goods is a large enough purchaser. The assumption behind this argument is that tariffs and quotas will decrease the demand for a product in world terms, so that its price falls. This is referred to as 'improving the terms of trade': it can be a successful policy only if the country imposing the tariffs or quotas is a very significant buyer in world terms of the goods or products affected.
- It is sometimes argued that restricting imports reduces a country's vulnerability to sudden price rises by foreign suppliers. Although this argument has some applicability in the case of oil, two points need to be made. Firstly, a country can only impose tariffs and quotas on imports to protect its vulnerability from sudden price rises if it can produce the goods subject to tariffs and quotas itself. Secondly, oil production is a unique case both because of its importance and because of the world percentage of oil production that comes from the Middle East. It could be argued that the

oil-producing countries of the Middle East are an example of an oligopoly.

Trade Policy Developments

In 1947 the USA signed the GATT agreement, the General Agreement on Tariffs and Trade, which was based on the principle that participating countries would reduce the restrictions on trade as a result of multilateral negotiation. The movement towards free trade within Europe began in earnest with the signing of the Treaty of Rome in 1957, which established a 'common market' for participating countries. The Treaty of Rome contained the following provisions: free trade among member states, a common tariff against goods imported into the EEC, and a common policy of agricultural price supports. The formation of the EEC has presented two major problems for the USA. Firstly, the USA is not a member of the EEC, so it must pay the common tariff imposed on imports; secondly, agricultural over-production within the EEC has led to EEC farm produce being exported at very low prices to traditional USA markets.

Partly as a response to the formation of the EEC, the Kennedy administration of the 1960's began the series of negotiations which became known as the Kennedy and Tokyo Rounds, which resulted in 1967 with an American commitment to reduce existing tariffs by an average of one-third. A further agreement in 1979 led to a second reduction in tariffs by one-third, to be achieved by stages during the 1980's. A persistent feature of Japanese trade policy throughout the 1980's was the imposition of quality controls and standards on imported goods, which had the effect of banning imports into that country.

The Balance of Payments

As a result of international trade, countries acquire indebtedness to each other. The balance of payments shows the relationship between a country's indebtedness to other countries for imports, and its payments from them for exports. The international trade account is made up of three groups of payments and receipts; the visible balance of trade, invisible items and capital movements.

The largest of the three groups payments is visible items in the balance of trade, represented by payments made and received for the receipt and sale of raw materials and manufactured goods. Since 1890 the trend has been for Britain to import a greater value of goods than it exports, although the value of North Sea Oil exports in the 1980's has tempered this tendency to an adverse balance.

Although Britain has usually had a deficit where visible earnings are concerned, it has usually had a surplus on invisible earnings, which are payments for services. Invisible items include the following:

- Shipping and civil aviation: Britain's earnings from civil aviation have more than compensated for the decline in its shipping tonnage since the 1960's.
- Financial services: London is still a very important financial centre, providing banking and insurance facilities which contribute significantly to annual earnings.
- Foreign investments also contribute significantly to invisible earnings.
- International tourism produces income for Britain, as the value of foreign visitors generally exceeds the sum spent by British residents' travelling abroad.

The third group of items of which the international balance of payments is made up, is capital movements. The income from foreign investments is received as a credit, whilst the original investment is represented as a payment. A change in the relative value of sterling to other currencies can have far-reaching economic consequences, possibly turning what would have been a balance of payments surplus into a deficit.

In world terms there is an overall balance between receipts and payments, although in the short-term a specific country's own account may either be in surplus or in deficit. The following problems can arise when a country's balance of payments is in surplus:

- Domestic living standards are held down, as the surplus could be spent on goods and services instead of being retained in the form of foreign currency.
- The surplus may contribute to demand-pull inflation in a period of full employment, as a result of the surplus's injection into the economy. Monetarists argue that a surplus contributes to inflation by increasing the money supply.
- The surplus may encourage further imports of manufactured goods from abroad, causing a run-down in the domestic economy.

- A surplus in one country will be experienced as a deficit in other countries: the deficit countries may resort to trade barriers as a form of defence, thus reducing the total quantity of world trade.

The following are the commonest responses to a balance of payments deficit:

- A balance of payments deficit may be met by reducing demand for foreign imports either through fiscal or monetary mechanisms. Such a policy avoids the criticism that the imposition of direct barriers to trade would bring, but can have serious economic consequences, particularly where unemployment is concerned.
- A balance of payments deficit may be met by devaluation or depreciation of the domestic currency, both of which will make imports more expensive. Devaluation occurs when the price of the domestic currency is dropped if the nation is operating a fixed exchange rate. Depreciation occurs when a country allows the external value of its currency to decline, when it is operating a 'floating' exchange rate.

Foreign Exchange

The Theory of Exchange Rates

From 1870 until 1914 Britain's exchange rates were on the Gold Standard: this meant that the price of one ounce of gold was fixed by law. During this period paper currency was fully convertible into gold. Between 1925 and 1931 Britain adopted a gold bullion standard, which meant that gold became available in bullion form for foreign trade only.

The effect of the gold standard on a country's balance of payments is that there is automatic action to rectify a balance of payments surplus or deficit, through the movement of gold into or out of a country. A deficit results in a reduction of the money supply, a contraction of the economy and rising unemployment, all of which decrease the domestic demand for imports, which become relatively more expensive although maintaining their absolute value in terms of gold. A deficit having this effect also makes the price of exports relatively cheap, thus increasing the demand for them and so contributing to a restoration of the balance of payment equilibrium.

Since the 1970's 'floating' as opposed to 'fixed' exchange rates have become the norm. The advantages of floating exchange rates are:

- Where a country's balance of payment is in disequilibrium, the exchange rate changes: a balance of payments surplus is met by automatic appreciation of the currency, and a deficit by automatic depreciation.
- A floating exchange rate affects the external value of a currency, unlike the gold standard, which affects the internal value of a currency as well.

The principal disadvantages of a floating exchange rate are:

- It produces uncertainty since the rate of exchange changes daily.
- It may encourage speculators to move from one currency to another in the hope of making a profit, thus contributing further to fluctuations in the exchange rate.

When a country's exchange rate is fixed, as with the Gold Standard, it is easy to determine the value of its currency. With a floating exchange rate, however, this becomes more difficult. One way of estimating a currency's value is by comparing it with several other currencies, each of which is weighted according to its trading importance to the currency under consideration. This gives rise to a trade weighted index.

Summary

1) International trade is based on the theory of comparative advantage. Its main assumptions are that perfect competition exists between nations, uninhibited by restrictions to trade imposed by governments in the form of tariffs or import quotas.

2) The balance of payments shows the relationship between the value of a nation's imports and the value of its exports. It consists of visible items, invisible items and capital movements.

3) Exchange rates may be fixed, as in the case of the Gold Standard, where there is automatic action to rectify a disequilibrium: or 'floating' where the rate of exchange changes daily in response to a balance of payments surplus or deficit.

Self-Assessment Test Eight – Questions

1) What are the three geographical factors which influence a country's forms of production?

2) What are the four assumptions on which the theory of trade is based?

3) What are the three groups of payments included in a nation's balance of payments?

4) What is the principal disadvantage in the way a fixed exchange rate corrects a surplus or deficit in the balance of payments?

Self-Assessment Test Eight – Answers

1) a) the location of mineral deposits

b) variations in climatic and soil conditions

c) development of special skills in the production of specific commodities

2) a) perfect competition between nations

b) full employment

c) no currency restrictions

d) no barriers to trade

3) a) visible items

b) invisible items

c) capital movements

4) it does so by affecting the level of internal economic activity.

Past Examination Questions on These Topics

1) What arguments do economists use to justify free international trade? Why, in practice, are there so many restrictions imposed by governments on international trade?

2) With regard to the theory of international trade, explain what is meant by:

a) absolute advantage

b) comparative advantage

c) the terms of trade

d) the balance of trade

e) the balance of payments

3) Under what circumstances may a country continue to import goods of a greater value than the value of goods it exports?

4) What factors determine the level of exports of a country?

5) In what way may the government attempt to correct an unfavourable balance of payments?

6) Discuss the methods which may be used by the government to correct an unfavourable balance of payments.

7) a) Explain how countries can benefit by applying the principle of comparative advantage in international trade.

b) Explain the circumstances in which a country might be justified in restricting i) imports ii) exports.

8) What are the arguments for and against the adoption of:

a) floating and

b) fixed rates of exchange?

9) 'When floating exchange rates are adopted, there is no balance of payments disequilibrium.' To what extent is this true?

9

Money and Banking

Objectives

After reading this chapter, you should be able to:

- Outline the Quantity Theory of Money
- List the Main Characteristics of J.M. Keynes' explanation of the demand for money
- Distinguish between cost-push inflation, demand-pull inflation and monetary inflation
- Describe the main functions of banks
- Describe the main functions of the Bank of England

Money and Banking

Money

The Uses of Money

Although primitive societies operate a simple economic system based on barter and payment-in-kind for goods and services, the development of money as the principal medium of exchange confers the following advantages:

- Money wages allow the individual to buy the quantity and assortment of goods or services he requires, at the price which provides him with the greatest satisfaction.
- Money wages facilitate the division of labour, allowing individuals to specialise.
- Money facilitates the arrangements for borrowing, as it allows the borrower command over the real resources of his choice.
- Money facilitates saving, thus allowing investment to become possible.

Money performs four main functions in a modern economy. Firstly, it is a medium of exchange. Secondly, it acts both as a measure of value and as a unit of account. In some economies, such as the black market in the Soviet Union, a foreign currency may be used as the unit of account, if confidence in the domestic currency is low. Although the measure of value of a product or service is always subjective, the money-price of goods is still a reflection of demand. The third function of money is to allow the building up of a store of value, by foregoing current consumption. This makes it possible for individuals to reserve some portion of their purchasing power for the future. Fourthly, money allows contracts to be agreed about the future spending of money and the future delivery of products or services.

Money and Value

Even if a distinction is made between money and value, the latter being regarded as the subjective estimate of the worth of products or services, it is still possible to regard market prices as an indication of the relative monetary value of products and services. The value of money itself declines when prices rise, as more money is then required to purchase the same quantity of products or services. Therefore:

- The price of a product or service is the amount of money that must be exchanged for it.
- The value of money is the quantity of products or services which it will purchase.

When examining the movement of prices over time, economists distinguish between three kinds of price movement. These are the long period movement of prices, the medium period movement of prices, and the short period movement of prices. The value of money tends to decline in the long period, as prices rise.

Several theories have been suggested to account for the changing value of money. In the Seventeenth Century it was argued that the greater the quantity of money in the economy, the more prices would rise. This quantity theory of money was resurrected in the 1920's by Professor Irving Fisher, who modified it by introducing the concept of the velocity of monetary circulation. Fisher's argument, expressed in the formula below, was that if money circulates quickly within a given period, that is equivalent to an increase in the total quantity of money in the economy. Fishe's theory can be stated thus;

$$MV = PT$$

where M = quantity of money in the economy
V = velocity of circulation of each unit of money
MV = total amount of money used in a given period
P = price level
T = volume of transactions in a given period.

The equation illustrates that the price level and the value of money are both influenced by the quantity of money, the rate at which money circulates, and the volume of products and services. Prices therefore rise if the velocity of money increases, or remain stable when the amount of money increases if this is accompanied by a proportional rise in output.

The Quantity Theory has been criticised on several grounds. It has been said that the formula only expresses that the total amount of money equals the value of total trade transactions multiplied by their average price. It has also been argued that the four variables in the equation are not independent variables: a change in M will usually bring about a change in either, or both, V and T. Finally,it has been pointed out that the Quantity Theory looks at the value of money only from the perspective of supply, and ignores the influence of demand: and that it also leaves out of account the influence of the interest rate on the value of money.

The Money Supply and the Demand for Money

Although it may be tempting to apply supply and demand analysis to the value of money, money is not directly comparable to other products. Firstly, the supply of money is not related to its cost of production. Secondly, the expression 'demand for money' means the demand to hold money, rather than invest it.

There are two kinds of money in use in a modern economy: cash in the form of bank-notes and currency, and money held in banking accounts which is transferable by cheque. Money held in banks forms approximately four-fifths of the total amount of money in Britain. The demand for money is subject to a number of influences, the chief of which are, according to the economist J.M. Keynes:

- the transactions motive: individuals require a holding of money to meet their everyday expenditure.
- the precautionary motive: individuals like to be able to use some of their holding of money to meet unexpected situations.
- the speculative motive: individuals are likely to hold more money if they think that prices of equities are likely to fall in the future, and less if they think prices are likely to rise. The amount of money held is therefore dependent on the interest rate.

Inflation

When prices are rising, business activity is stimulated, and because production is carried on in anticipation of demand and not all the costs of production respond immediately to rising prices, profits will be greater. When prices are falling, however, there is a danger that profits will disappear altogether as the costs of production do not respond immediately to the fall in prices. Output is therefore increased when prices rise, and decreased when prices fall.

Price changes affect income groups in different ways. Those living on fixed incomes are adversely affected by rising prices, whilst those who rely on profits are adversely affected by falling prices. There is a tendency for the incomes of wage-earners to lag behind a rise in prices, but to follow such a rise eventually. It should be noted that changes in price levels have an effect on the way national income is distributed between the three groups.

The term inflation has the following meanings:

- An increase in the money supply: when the Central Bank increases the quantity of money the general level of prices will rise, if the level of output is not increased proportionately to match the increase in the money supply.
- An unstable economic condition in which growth in the quantity of money persistently exceeds growth in the level of output of products and services, so that prices are constantly rising to keep pace with demand.
- The term 'hyper-inflation' is used when the excess in the money supply creates huge price increases.

Economists disagree about the causes of inflation, three main explanations of it being proposed:

- Cost-push inflation. This occurs when increases in the costs of production push up prices. Some analysts believe that trade unions have contributed to inflation by wage claims in excess of levels of production. It is also believed that rising import costs contribute to inflation, as does depreciation in the value of the domestic currency against foreign currencies. The tendency of some firms to base their prices inflexibly on a standard increase on costs also contributes to inflation.
- Demand-pull inflation. This occurs when aggregate demand exceeds the value of output. Demand cannot be met by the volume of output, and so it is met by rising prices.
- Monetary inflation. This occurs when there has been too great an increase in the money stock. Proponents of this view argue that the sole cause of inflation is an excessive increase in the money stock.

Banking

The Banking System

The following kinds of banking institutions exist in Britain:

- Bank of England. This is the central bank, acting on behalf of the government and the other banks, and as a lender of last resort to the commercial banks, as well as supervising the entire banking system through the Board of Banking Supervision, established under the Banking Act 1987.
- Commercial Banks. These are the banks which handle most individuals' banking matters. In Britain these banks provide a comprehensive range of services including the provision of business loans and mortgages.
- Building Societies. Although most building societies concentrate on providing mortgages for house-buyers, there has been a tendency, since the Building Societies Act, 1986, for them to expand their activities considerably.
- Merchant Banks. These institutions concentrate on arranging finance for large companies.

Banks have the following functions:

- Banks accept deposits of money, and pay interest on these. The interest rate paid by banks on deposits is usually 2% below the Bank of England's minimum lending rate.
- Banks act as agents for payment for their customers, through the chequing system.
- Banks make loans to both businesses and private customers. This is the second most significant function of banking.

The Relationship between Bank Loans and Bank Deposits

Bank loans increase the quantity of money in an economy, and also increase the amount of money that is deposited with banks. If a bank lends a sum of money to individual A to pay for a service performed by individual B, the payment made to B will be deposited with a bank, thus increasing the total amount deposited with banks. Banks also create deposits by purchasing government securities, a form of loan to the government. The banks' ability to create their own deposits by expanding credit and thus the total quantity of money in the economy, is of enormous economic significance.

Although the banks create their own deposits, there are limits placed on their expansion of credit. If an individual bank supplies more credit than is consistent with general bank policy, only a small percentage of the additional deposits created will remain with it, the rest being paid into accounts held at other banks. This could result in the bank concerned having to go into its reserves at the Bank of England in order to meet its obligations to other banks.

Cheques

The most common form of payment in business is the cheque. There are two ways in which cheques are cleared by the banks. If a cheque is paid to an account at the same bank as the one on which it is drawn, the clearing process is carried out internally by the bank itself; this is known as inter-bank or head office clearing. All other cheques which involve the transfer of funds from one bank to another are processed by the Committee of London and Scottish banks, which is made up of the main high street banks. The total amount of money to be transferred as a result of all transactions is calculated on a daily basis, and funds are transferred from each of the banks' accounts with the Banking Department of the Bank of England. This process normally takes about three working days to complete from the date of receipt of a cheque. The introduction of CHAPS (Clearing Houses Automated System) has improved the speed of the clearing process. Standing orders and direct debits are now processed by BACS (Bankers' Automated Clearing Services), through which many company employees are now paid.

The Balance Sheet

The most important characteristic of a bank is that it is prepared to lend more cash than it holds at any one time. A bank's willingness to lend money is, however, inhibited by its need to produce cash on demand for its customers, and by the knowledge that an expansion of bank lending will increase the demand for cash, although not all loans require to be supported by cash. A bank knows from experience the proportion of bank assets that must be kept in liquid form to meet the demand for cash in normal circumstances, but it must be prepared to meet exceptional demand without undue delay and without loss. A bank has to balance the need for liquidity against the desire to lend money and invest it.

The balance sheet of a bank lists the following as liabilities: capital, reserves, and deposits on current and deposit account. Bank deposits are by far the greatest liability of the banks, and are of very great economic significance because they represent the greater part of the economy's total purchasing power. Bank deposits increase when the terms of credit are easy, and grow more slowly when the terms of credit are harder to obtain.

A bank's assets are the amounts which it is owed by individuals, businesses, other financial institutions and the government. A bank's assets are distributed in such a way that it is able both to pay cash on demand and make a profit. Liquid assets are less profitable, as a general rule, than other forms of assets.

A bank's reserve of cash in the form of coins and notes forms a very small percentage of its total assets, as cash holdings earn no interest. Cash ratio deposits are determined by the Bank of England, which requires that banks keep 0.5% of their eligible liabilities in cash at the Bank of England. Market loans are made up of loans made by the banks to the London money market: banks are obliged to keep 5% of eligible liabilities in the money markets and 2% with discount houses. The discount market is money lent to the London Discount Market Association (LDMA) at call or at short notice, either on an overnight basis or for a period up to 14 days. Other than the cash held at the Bank of England, these are the most liquid assets held by banks, and will be called upon when the banks require cash.

Other banking assets include loans made and received from other members of the monetary sector, and certificates of cash deposits; the latter are negotiable instruments given to large depositors who have left funds with the banks for a fixed period. Many banks also lend money through the money market to local authorities. Treasury Bills are sold on a weekly basis to the discount houses, and some of these are then purchased by banks. Bills of exchange are issued by large companies to provide finance for trade, and are sold through the money market. These assets also provide banks with liquidity should they require it.

Another form of assets owned by the banks are their holdings in British government stocks, known as 'gilt-edged' securities. The banks buy these stocks in such a way that a certain proportion of them mature each week, thus providing income on a weekly basis. Banks also derive income from advances made to business and personal customers in the form of overdrafts and loans, these providing the greatest source of banking income.

The Control of Banking

The Banking Act 1979 introduced for the first time a strong measure of statutory control over the banking industry. Its provisions were strengthened by the Credit Unions Act 1979 and the Banking Act 1987. The legislation provides for:

- Bank licensing: all deposit-taking institutions must be licensed by the Bank of England, the licenses being in two forms. An institution licensed as a bank must have substantial funds and either offer a wide range of services or specialise in a particular form of banking. An institution licensed as a deposit-taker may offer fewer services than a bank.
- Only recognised banks and named institutions may use the title bank or banker. Foreign banks operating under the laws of their own country may describe themselves as banks.
- The banks are required to pay a small amount of their funds into the deposit protection scheme which is designed to protect small depositors in the wake of a bank failure.

The Bank of England and Monetary Policy

The Role of the Bank of England

The Bank of England has two major departments, the Issue Department which is responsible for the issue of notes, and the Banking Department which is responsible for the Bank's other activities. The main characteristics of the Bank of England are the following:

- It acts as the government's banker, receiving government revenues and paying government bills.
- It acts as banker to the other banks, holding their balances and reserves. It also acts as the lender of last resort to the other banks.
- It supervises the banking system, and implements the government's monetary policy.

The Balance Sheet of the Bank of England

The Balance sheet of the Bank of England is divided into two halves, the first of which sets out the business of the Issue Department, the second being concerned with the business of the Banking Department. It will be convenient to summarise the balance sheet of the Issue Department first:

- Notes in circulation, including the comparatively small amount of notes issued by the Scottish and Northern Irish banks.
- Notes in the Banking Department which have been sold by the Issue Department.
- Government securities held by the Issue Department to support the issue of notes.

The balance sheet of the Banking Department of the Bank of England contains details of the following liabilities and assets:

- Liabilities include government deposits, special deposits relating to the Bank's special function as operator of the government's monetary policy, and the deposits of other banks, and reserves.
- Assets include government securities, advances to other institutions, and the notes and coins which the Bank of England supplies to other banks.

Monetary Policy

The Bank of England has the power to contract or expand the volume of purchasing power in Britain by its influence on the commercial banks. Although the Bank of England will usually implement monetary policies that have been decided upon by the Treasury, the Bank has considerable influence on the government's choice of monetary policy. The traditional instruments of monetary policy are outlined below:

- Open Market Operations. The Bank of England can control the commercial banks' cash and liquid assets ratios, as a way of influencing the banking system's total credit and deposit creating ability. It does this by buying or selling government securities on the open market.
  If the Bank of England wishes to contract the money supply, it may do so by selling government securities to the public, whose payment for these is made by cheques drawn on commercial

banks: commercial banks' deposits are thereby reduced. A further contraction of the money supply may occur if the commercial banks have been operating close to their desired ratio of liquid assets to total deposits. They may act to restore their level of liquid assets to total deposits by reducing lending.

If the Bank of England wishes to expand the money supply, it may do so by purchasing securities from the public, paying for these by cheques drawn on itself. This will have the effect of increasing the volume of money in the commercial banking system, allowing banks to increase the amount of credit they give to customers.

Open market operations may have a greater effect on interest rates, than on the volume of bank deposits and the money supply. Contractionary open market operations are frequently used to increase interest rates, when the government wishes to reduce the demand for bank credit.

– Interest rates. A second means by which the Bank of England can manipluate the public demand for bank credit, is through the Bank of England's own lending rate. In the post-war period up until 1970 government monetary policy was predominantly 'Keynesian'. The main intention of successive governments was to manipulate aggregate demand through the interst rate, and little emphasis was given to control of the money supply. During the 1980's, British monetary policy was 'monetarist' in character. The main intention of government policy was to control inflation, the principal cause of which was seen as the excess supply of money in the economy.

Summary

1) J.M. Keynes thought that the demand for money was influenced by three main motives: the transactions motive, the precautionary motive, and the speculative motive.

2) There are three main explanations of inflation. These are cost-push inflation, demand-pull inflation and monetary inflation.

3) Banks have the following important functions: they accept deposits of money, act as agents of payment for their customers, and make loans available to customers.

4) The Bank of England acts as the government's banker, as the lender of last resort to other banks, supervises the banking system, and implements the government's monetary policy.

Self-Assessment Test Nine – Questions

1) According to J.M. Keynes, what are the three main influences on the demand for money?

2) What are the three main explanations of inflation?

3) What are the three main functions of banks?

4) What are the three main characteristics of the Bank of England?

Self-Assessment Test Nine – Answers

1) a) the transactions motive

b) the precautionary motive

c) the speculative motive

2) a) cost-push inflation

b) demand-pull inflation

c) monetary inflation

3) a) they accept deposits of money

b) they act as agents of payment for their customers

c) they make loans to customers

4) a) it is the government's banker

b) it is a lender of last resort for other banks

c) it supervises the banking system, and implements the government's monetary policy

Past Examination Questions on These Topics

1) Distinguish between fiscal and monetary policies. Discuss whether it is possible to use one to the exclusion of the other.

2) Why do people hold money balances if money is only useful when it can be exchanged for goods or services?

3) What limits the power of a commercial bank to create credit?

4) Explain two of the following concepts:

a) the demand for money

b) the creation of bank deposits

c) control of the money supply

5) What are the major causes of inflation?

6) What is the role of a Central Bank?

7) a) What is 'money' in a modern economy?

b) What are the functions of money?

c) Suggest the likely effects on each function of changes in the value of money.

10

Macroeconomics

10

Macroeconomics

Objectives

After reading this chapter, you should be able to:

- Explain how the classical theorists believed that aggregate demand could be predicted more certainly than the demand curve for an individual product
- Explain the fundamental point of difference regarding unemployment, between J.M. Keynes and the classical theorists
- Explain what is meant by the marginal propensity to consume and the marginal propensity to save

Macroeconomics

The Classical View of Aggregate Supply and Aggregate Demand

When considering aggregate supply and aggregate demand one cannot assume that the aggregate supply and demand curves follow the same directions of slope as supply and demand curves for an individual product. This is because the demand curve for an individual product is drawn on the assumption that demand changes as the price of one product changes relative to the price of other products. Aggregate demand curves, however, represent the movement of all prices, so that a fall in the general level of prices does not make switching between products advantageous: there are no 'other products' in the aggregate demand curve. In the case of the supply curves for an individual product, it is assumed that supply changes as the price of the individual product relative to other products changes. In aggregate supply, however, a producer cannot switch from other products, because once again there are no 'other products' in the aggregate supply curve.

The classical economists argued that the aggregate demand curve will respond to changes in average price levels in the way depicted on the graph below. They reasoned that if average prices fall by a given percentage, purchasing power is increased, which increases the quantity of goods and services demanded. The classical economists believed that demand would increase by approximately the same amount as the decrease in average prices. For the classical economists the aggregate demand curve could therefore be drawn more accurately than the demand curve for an individual product, where the proportion between price changes and changes in demand varies, both for the same product and between products. The crucial point about aggregate demand from the classical perspective is that demand is perceived as being dependent on the quantity and purchasing power of money.

The classical economists saw the aggregate supply curve as vertical at the potential or full employment quantity of output. They argued that aggregate supply must be vertical because of the following: if the economy is at point B initially, with full employment, a change in the level of prices, including labour, will not affect supply, as prices will not have changed their positions relative to each other. If prices move to C, for example, wages and other prices are still in the same relative positions they were before, the only change being an increase in money. Therefore, point C on the graph must be directly above point B.

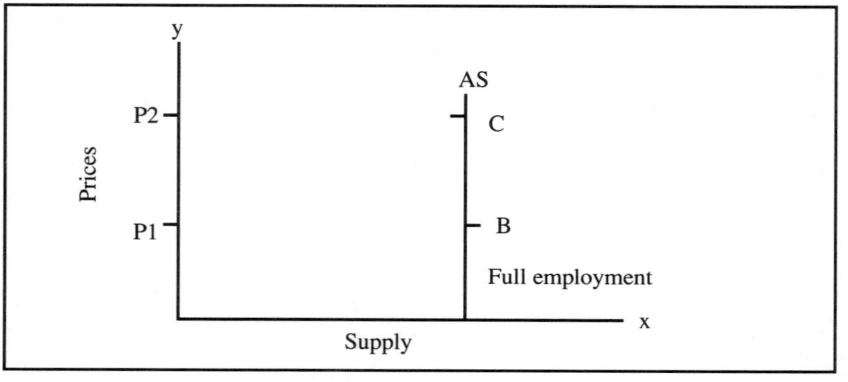

The classical economists believed that the economy would be led by market forces to a natural equilibrium where the aggregate demand curve would intersect the aggregate supply curve at full employment, as the graph below shows. They believed that market forces would act

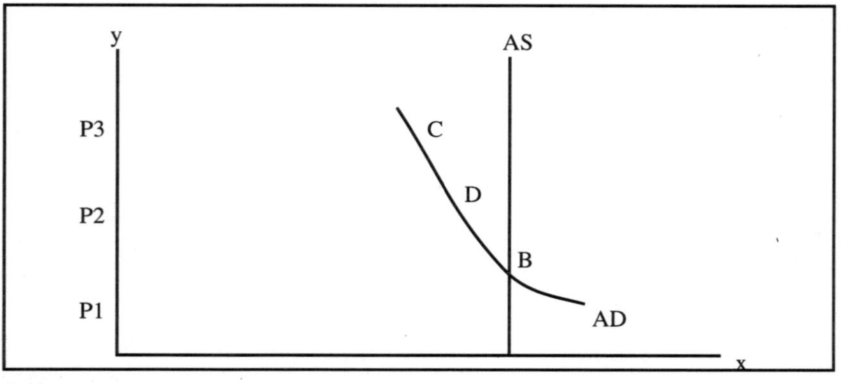

to diminish unemployment in the following way. Unemployment occurs when the aggregate demand for goods and services at the initial price is less than it would be at the full employment output. According to the classical view suppliers will drop their prices in order to stimulate demand, and wages will fall as unemployed people become willing to accept lower wages. As prices and money wages fall, the purchasing power of money increases, increasing demand. Movement along the demand curve will be from positions C and D towards the natural equilibrium B, from where there will be no further downward pressure on prices and wages.

The classical economists emphasised the central importance of the quantity of money and its purchasing power in their analysis of aggregate demand. They saw a change in the quantity of money as liable to result in a shift in aggregate demand: to the right, if the quantity of money increased, and to the left if it decreased. A classical explanation of an economic depression is illustrated in the graph below.

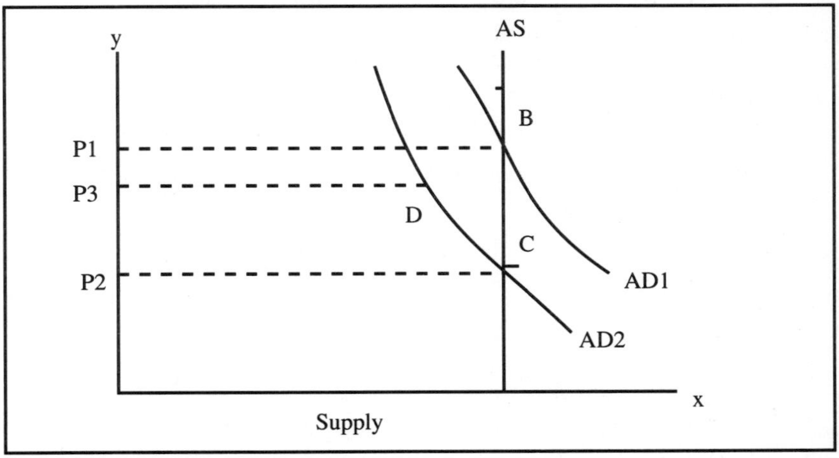

Aggregate demand shifts to the left as the result of a decrease in the quantity of money due, for example, to a crisis in the banking system. Full employment is still possible if prices and wages fall to C, but prices and wages remain high in the face of slack demand and unemployment, reaching only P_3 instead of P_2. Prices and wages are too high for the new equilibrium, so the amount of goods and services produced falls below the full employment equilibrium. In the classical view the economy would be eventually self-righting, if there was no further disturbance of market forces. The classical response offers two solutions for an economic depression:

- Restore the quantity of money by increasing the money supply, which would stimulate demand.
- Persuade employers and the work-force to accept lower wages and prices in order to move to the new equilibrium point quickly.

The Keynesian View of Aggregate Supply and Aggregate Demand

J.M. Keynes published his 'General Theory of Employment, Interest and Money' against the back-ground of mass unemployment in Britain and America in the 1930's. Keynes proposed the following:

- A market economy's equilibrium might not be one of full employment, but might consist of a considerable degree of unemployment, which Keynes called the 'unemployment equilibrium'. Furthermore, the market economy which did achieve full employment might be quite unstable.
- Keynes argued that unemployment is caused by an inadequate aggregate demand.
- Keynes proposed that the solution to unemployment was to increase aggregate demand by increasing government expenditure.

Unlike the classical economists, then, who saw the need to let market forces restore the economy to equilibrium, Keynes thought the government should take the necessary action.

The classical economists had argued that wages and prices might not respond immediately to a decrease in aggregate demand, and had suggested that this lack of response could result in periods of transitional large-scale unemployment, lasting until wages and prices fell. Keynes rejected the classical view, arguing that wages and prices would remain fixed indefinitely in the face of large-scale unemployment. The rigidity of prices and wages is illustrated in the line BC in the graph below. According to Keynes' theory, a fall in demand would result in a fall in supply, and not a fall in prices and wages. This is why Keynes proposed that aggregate demand be

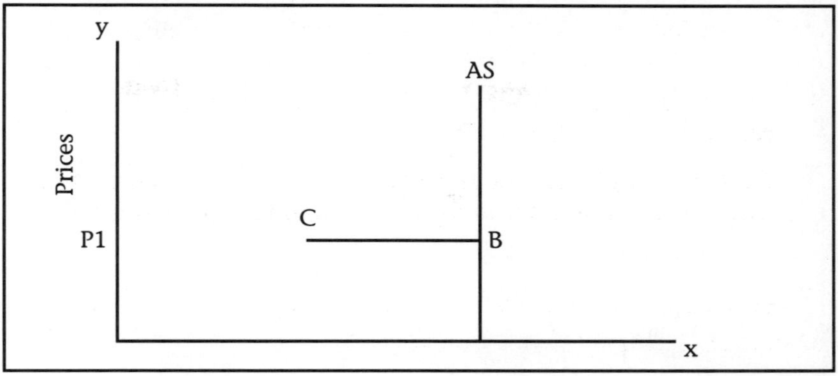

stimulated by government expenditure: this would result in increased production, and aggregate supply would move to the right along the line CB, towards full employment. It is important to realise that Keynes saw aggregate supply as having two ranges: a horizontal range which comes into prominence during periods of depression and recession, and a vertical range which comes into prominence when aggregate demand is sufficient to produce full employment.

Keynes suggested that aggregate demand be analysed by studying the following elements of national product:

- Personal consumption expenditures
- Investment demand
- Government purchases of goods and services
- Net exports

In Keynes' opinion, the Great Depression was caused by the collapse of aggregate demand, particularly investment demand.

Equilibrium with Unemployment

Keynes' fundamental argument that the economy may reach an equilibrium with large-scale unemployment can most simply be considered by an examination of an economy in which there are only two components of aggregate demand: personal consumption expenditure and investment demand.

Personal consumption is based on disposable income. The ratio of consumption to disposable income is different for a low-income individual than for a high-income individual. The former may consume more than his disposable income by borrowing in order to meet the basic needs of everyday life: whilst the latter will be able to divide his disposable income between consumption and saving. This is illustrated in the graph below:

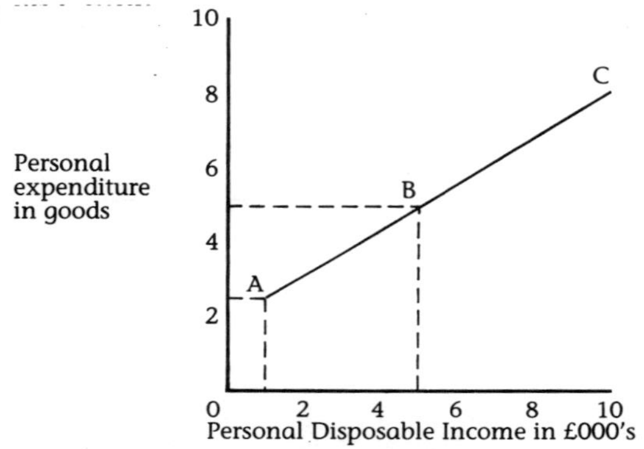

As can be seen from the graph, an individual with a disposable income of £1,000 p.a. actually spends £2,500 p.a. in order to meet the basic needs of everyday life, the extra sum coming from borrowing. Consumption, or personal expenditure, rises as disposable income rises, but the rate of increase of consumption slows down after reaching the break-even point B, where consumption and disposable income are equal. The relationship between consumption and disposable income is known as the consumption function, and is a central part of Keynes' theory. The break-even point can be identified by drawing a 45° line equidistant from the axes, so that the point of intersection where the line AC meets the 45° line will be B, where disposable income and consumption are equal. This is illustrated in the graph below.

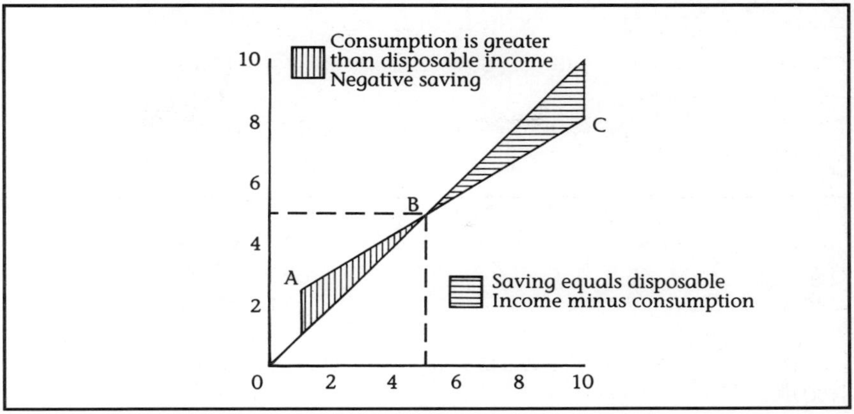

As well as constructing a graph to show the relationship between personal consumption and disposable income, one can use a graph to illustrate the relationship between an entire nation's consumption

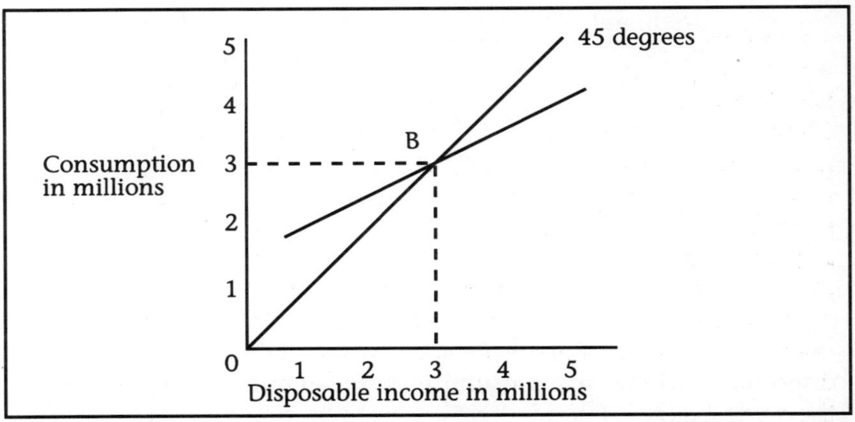

and its disposable income. In the imaginary example below a disposable national income of 3 billion pounds equals annual consumption of 3 billion pounds. As saving is the difference between disposable income and consumption, saving may be calculated by subtracting consumption from disposable income.

Keynes was concerned to discover the relationship between

consumption, saving and disposable income. The concept of the marginal propensity to consume is an important part of his theory.

$$\text{Marginal Propensity to Consume} = \frac{\text{Change in consumption}}{\text{Change in disposable income}}$$

$$\text{Marginal Propensity to Save} = \frac{\text{Change in saving}}{\text{Change in disposable income}}$$

The marginal propensity to consume is therefore that fraction of increased disposable income which is consumed: whilst the marginal propensity to save is that fraction of increased disposable income which is saved. Note that MPC + MPS = 1, as any increase in disposable income is either consumed or saved. Two other concepts emphasised by Keynes are that of the average propensity to consume, expressed as:

$$\text{APC} = \frac{\text{total consumption}}{\text{total income}}$$

and the average propensity to save, expressed as:

$$\text{APS} = \frac{\text{total savings}}{\text{total income}}$$

Keynes' argument that a free market economy might reach equilibrium with large-scale unemployment can most simply be demonstrated by considering an economy in which the following components have been excluded:

- international trade
- government spending
- depreciation
- no retention of business profits

In this example, therefore, Gross National Product, Net National Product, National Income and disposable income are all equal. In this imaginary economy there are just two components of aggregate demand: consumption expenditure and investment demand. In the table below an assumption is made that investment demand remains constant at £100 million.

GNP/NNP National Income, Disposable Income	Consumption Demand	Saving	Investment Demand	Aggregate Demand
1,000	1,000	0	100	1,100
1,500	1,400	100	100	1,500
2,000	1,800	200	100	1,900
2,500	2,300	200	100	2,400

Equilibrium occurs when aggregate demand equals national product; this is also the point where saving and investment demand are equal. At a higher rate of national product than £1,500 million, demand is inadequate. At £2,500 million, for example, there is a shortfall between aggregate demand and production: the excess in production is known as undesired inventory accumulation. Production decreases until it once again reaches equilibrium. It is important to distinguish here between investment demand and actual investment. Investment demand is the level of investment wanted by businesses: actual investment is the level attained, which may be greater or lesser than investment demand.

It is now possible to explain the central point of Keynes' theory, that the equilibrium national product need not be at the quantity necessary to guarantee full employment. The equilibrium national product may be at a lesser quantity than the full employment national product.

The Concept of the Multiplier

The graph below shows what happens when investment demand increases by £100 million. As can be seen, aggregate demand increases by the same amount, moving from AD to AD1: the equilibrium also moves, from B to C, where the new aggregate demand function intersects the 45 line. Note, however, that the aggregate demand increase of £100 million has resulted in an increase of £500 million in national product.

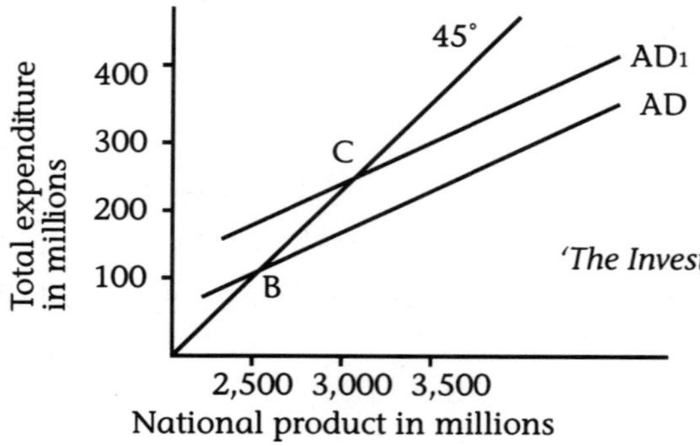

'The Investment Multiplier'

This 'multiplied' increase in national product is explained by the fact that increased investment produces not only more capital goods, but also increases incomes for those producing the capital goods, and thus expenditure on consumer goods. The investment multiplier can be defined as:

$$\text{Investment multiplier} = \frac{\text{change in equilibrium real national product}}{\text{change in investment demand}}$$

An increase in investment demand of £100 million produces an increase in national product of £500 million. If the MPC is 0.8, consumption will be increased by £80 million, and saving by £20 million. The £80 million spent by consumers goes to producers in the form of income, and thus back into national income in wages: where it is again spent by consumers with an MPC of 0.8, this time £64 million being consumed and £16 million being saved. This process is repeated in a chain of payments between consumers and producers. The more steeply the consumption function slopes, the greater will be the multiplier effect of an increase in investment demand. This is expressed as:

$$\text{Multiplier} = \frac{1}{\text{1-MPC}} \qquad \text{or Multiplier} = \frac{1}{\text{MPS}}$$

The multiplier effect works in the other direction as well, when investment demand decreases.

It is important to realise that the multiplier effect may take a considerable time to work its way through the economy, and can therefore be seen as one of the major contributors to economic disequilibrium.

Summary

1) The classical theorists believed that market forces would establish a natural equilibrium where the aggregate demand curve would intersect the aggregate supply curve at full employment.

2) J.M. Keynes argued that a market economy could establish equilibrium at large scale unemployment.

3) J.M. Keynes argued that governments have a responsibility to increase aggregate demand during a period of depression by increasing government expenditure.

Self-Assessment Test Ten – Questions

1) Why did the classical theorists believe that the aggregate demand could be predicted more certainly than the demand curve for an individual product?

2) According to the classical theorists, on what is aggregate demand dependent?

3) What was the fundamental point of difference regarding employment, between J.M. Keynes and the classical theorists?

4) What is the solution to unemployment, according to Keynes?

5) Define:

a) marginal propensity to consume

b) marginal propensity to save

Self-Assessment Test Ten – Answers

1) Aggregate demand responds exactly to a rise or fall in price, where an individual demand curve may have a varying response to price changes.

2) The quantity and purchasing power of money.

3) The classical theorists believed that market forces would establish a natural equilibrium where the aggregate demand curve would intersect the aggregate supply curve at full employment. Keynes believed that a market economy could establish equilibrium at large-scale unemployment.

4) Increase aggregate demand by increasing government expenditure.

5) a) $\text{MPC} = \dfrac{\text{Change in consumption}}{\text{Change in disposable income}}$

b) $\text{MPS} = \dfrac{\text{Change in saving}}{\text{Change in disposable income}}$

Past Examination Questions on These Topics

1) Define consumption, saving and investment and explain how they are related.

2) Give reasons why the free market economy may not achieve the optimum allocation of resources.

3) a) Distinguish between the equilibrium level of national income and the full employment level of national income.

b) Explain why, in a market economy, they may differ.

11

The Economic Role of the Government

Objectives

After reading this chapter, you should be able to:

- List the four canons of taxation
- Distinguish between progressive and regressive taxation

The Economic Role of the Government

Government Policy Objectives

Although some politicians speak as if minimal government intervention in the economy was the most desirable objective of government economic policy, all governments in industrialised societies play a significant role in determining economic activity. In particular, government objectives include the following:

- the maintenance of employment levels
- the control of inflation
- the maintenance of a favourable balance of payments
- the encouragement of economic growth
- the maintenance of public services

There are three main ways in which governments are able to implement their policy objectives. Firstly, a government can influence the direction of the economy through taxation and government spending. Secondly, a government can influence the direction of the economy through the supply and price of money. Thirdly, a government can influence the direction of the economy by direct intervention, an example of which is the government establishment of a prices and incomes policy.

Fiscal Policy

A government needs to raise taxes in order to provide for national defence and the maintenance of internal law and order. It also needs to raise taxes to pay for those welfare services, provided by the state, including education, social services environmental services and subsidies to nationalised and privately-owned industries. The extent of government taxation will be partly determined by the degree to which essential services are owned or financed by the state. The second main reason for the raising of taxes is to curtail consumer demand in the economy, so that the factors of production can be used to satisfy the government's public sector requirements. In addition to these two major reasons for taxation, a government raises taxes to accomplish the following ends:

- To limit the consumption of harmful products such as alcohol and tobacco, or products harmful to the environment.
- To re-distribute labour, through tax concessions or disincentives.
- To re-distribute incomes as a result of social policy. The re-distribution of income was one of the most important aims of fiscal policy in Britain in the period immediately following the Second World War.

According to Adam Smith, there are four canons of taxation. Taxes should be equal, in the sense that they are proportionate to income. Secondly, there must be certainty about the amount of taxation to be paid. Thirdly, there should be convenience of payment and collection. Fourthly, taxes should be economical, in the sense that their cost of collection is not excessive. The principle of proportionality has been modified by modern governments, so that the amount of taxes paid by the rich increases more than proportionately in relation to income. This kind of taxation is known as 'progressive' taxation.

In Britain taxation is organised in the following way:

- Direct taxation consists of income tax, based on individual earnings: corporation tax, which is levied on the profits of companies: taxes payable on the transfer of capital, such as capital gains tax and death duties: and national insurance, which is a proportional tax on income. Direct taxes account for well over 50% of all government revenue.
- Indirect taxation consists of taxation on expenditure rather than income and includes: Value Added Tax (VAT), currently fixed at two rates in Britain, zero-rate and 15%: customs duty levied on goods coming into the country: and excise duty levied on the amount of a commodity subject to the tax, rather than on the price of the commodity as in the case of VAT. Indirect taxes are regarded as regressive, because they consume a larger proportion of the incomes of the lower-paid.

In April 1990 domestic rates in England and Wales were abolished, and a Community Charge or Poll Tax introduced. The

Community Charge is an example of regressive taxation, because each individual is liable for the same amount regardless of income.

The Incidence of Taxation.

The 'incidence' of taxation is upon the individual who pays the tax. This is most clear in the case of income tax, where the incidence is always on the individual whose income is taxed, because income tax is not transferable to someone else. In the case of indirect taxation such as VAT, however, it may not be clear whether the incidence of the tax will fall on the buyer or the seller of a product, or be divided between them. This will depend on the elasticity of demand for the product in question. If a product priced at £5.00 is made subject to a tax of £1.00 the incidence of the tax is on the purchaser, who must now pay £6.00 for the product. If demand for the product is perfectly inelastic the incidence remains with the purchaser, as demand is unaffected by the increase in price. If demand for the product is perfectly elastic, however, the incidence of the tax falls on the producer, as demand for the product declines in response to the increase in price caused by the tax.

Listed below are some of the commonest effects of taxation on economic activity.

- Heavy direct taxation can act as a deterrent to work, making over-time seen unprofitable. Heavy indirect taxation, on the other hand, may be an incentive to work, as individuals strive to earn the extra money they require for goods that have been made more expensive by indirect taxation. In 1979 the Conservative government reduced the level of income tax and increased the rate of VAT in order to stimulate economic growth.
- Increased taxation can deter saving, as more disposable income is required to meet everyday expenses. Increases in indirect taxation do not deter saving as much as increases in direct taxation.
- It is argued by some that taxes on profit discourage enterprise, and so reduce national production.
- Taxation may be used to create a surplus, in order to reduce an excessive supply of money in the economy, thus reducing inflation. An increase in indirect taxation can contribute to inflation by pushing up prices, which leads to an increase in the demand for wages.

The Government and Employment

The pursuit of full employment as a prime objective of government policy was stated by Lord Beveridge in 'Full Employment in a Free Society', (1944). Beveridge stated that there were four conditions that had to be met if full employment was to be reached. These conditions were:

- Adequate private and public expenditure to prevent a deficiency of demand.
- Planned location of industry to avoid structural unemployment resulting from localised industries.
- The organised mobility of labour.
- Moderate wage demands by the unions to avoid inflation.

Since the early 1980's government definitions of the unemployed have changed a number of times, so that establishing exactly what is meant by the term 'unemployment', or calculating its extent, has become difficult. Some analysts calculate the number of unemployed by counting the number of people in receipt of unemployment benefit or income support, but this leaves out of account those who are actively seeking for work but do not register for state benefits: many women fall into this category.

Beveridge defined full employment as a situation where no more than 3% of the working population were unemployed; and although the 3% definition became a very influential one, it took no account of regional pockets of unemployment. Another way of defining full employment is to calculate the number of job vacancies; if there are more job vacancies than unemployed people, it would be possible to say there was full employment. This approach, however, fails to take account of the fact that job vacancies may occur in regions some way away from concentrations of unemployment, as happened in Britain in the middle 1980's, when there were many job vacancies in the south of the country, but unemployment in the north of England was at record levels. It also fails to take account of the fact that there may not be a perfect match between the skills required to fill vacancies and the skills of the unemployed. Economists distinguish between the following kinds of unemployment:

- Cyclical unemployment occurs when there is a general deficiency of demand due to a trade depression. The term is derived from the phenomenon of the Nineteenth Century trade cycle.

- Frictional unemployment occurs when the labour-force cannot easily be transferred from one form of production to another, either because it lacks geographical or occupational mobility. Frictional unemployment may result from changes in taste or fashion or improvements in technology which make established forms of production redundant. When unemployment results from changes in the structure of the economy, it is called structural unemployment.
- Seasonal unemployment occurs when weather conditions reduce the demand for certain kinds of labour: it affects particularly the construction industry.
- Residual unemployment includes all those who remain unemployed because of illness or disability, or because of an unwillingness to work.

The Unemployment Debate

Until the latter half of the 1970's it was assumed that the most effective way to reduce unemployment was to run a budget deficit in order to boost demand. The idea then began to gain acceptance that demand-side policies contributed to the problem they were supposed to be solving because budget deficits caused inflation, itself a major cause of unemployment.

An alternative approach to the problem of unemployment is known as the supply-side approach. The fundamental principle of the supply-side approach is that the economy is self-regulating, if it is not subjected to government interference or trade union restrictive practices. Supply-side economics concentrates on the importance of reducing the costs of production as the principal means of controlling inflation and achieving full employment. Part of the approach is to argue that there is a natural level of unemployment, and that government attempts to interfere with unemployment levels are the principal cause of inflation. The supply-side theorists advocate the following policies to control unemployment. Firstly, a reduction of welfare payments so that these are well below the equilibrium wage rate for lower paid workers, on the grounds that generous unemployment benefits encourage unemployment. Secondly, a reduction of direct taxes. Thirdly, a reduction in the power of trade unions to impose immoderate pay settlements and restrictive practices on employers. Finally, the availability of job training schemes to improve the quality of the labour force and its occupational mobility.

Keynsian and Neo-Keynsian economists dispute the correctness of the supply-side approach, arguing that the real solution to unemployment lies in demand. They argue that budget deficits in times of high unemployment are unlikely to cause inflation, and that the state financing of public works can be partially met by a decrease in social security payments. They also contend that the money supply should be increased in periods of high unemployment by reducing interest rates, in order to stimulate demand and so reduce unemployment.

The Government and Inflation

Inflation can be defined as a rise in prices accompanied by a relative decline in the value of money. It is argued that inflation has the following consequences:

- By making imports relatively cheap and exports relatively expensive, inflation has an adverse effect on the balance of payments. Note that the effect of domestic inflation on the balance of payments depends on the domestic economy's rate of inflation as compared to the rate of inflation of trading partners overseas.
- A high rate of inflation may discourage savings because it increases uncertainty. High nominal rates of interest also discourage investment.
- Inflation reduces the real income of those living on pensions and fixed incomes because it reduces the value of money. Inflation increases the real income of people dependant on prices.

The Relationship between Inflation and Unemployment

It used to be commonly believed that inflation could be reduced only at the cost of an increase in unemployment, and that unemployment could only be reduced at the cost of increased inflation. This view changed as a result of research published by A.W.H. Phillips in 1962. The Phillips curve seemed to indicate that an unemployment rate of 5.5% would be accompanied by zero inflation. Phillips' research was based on examining the relationship between unemployment, inflation and wage rises in the British economy, during the period 1862-1958.

Monetarist economists have used the Phillips curve to argue that a reduction in inflation would bring about a reduction in unemployment, and this belief was one of the underlying principles of the Conservative government's economic policy in the period following 1979.

Milton Friedman argued that in the short run it was possible to expand the money supply in order to reduce unemployment, but that in the long run unemployment would rise to its natural level, accompanied by an increase in inflation. His argument was based on the idea that an expansion of the money supply causes an immediate increase in prices but has no immediate effect on wages. The demand for labour increases as its real cost has declined relative to prices, so that more people are drawn into the labour market, which begins to increase its money wages. A short-term equilibrium is reached, in which inflation has successfully reduced unemployment: but as soon as the labour-force realises that real incomes are still below money incomes, the demand for wages once more increases, and the supply curve of labour returns to its original position. Friedman's theory is based on the money illusion, the tendency of people to assume that an increase in money wages is equivalent to an increase in real wages.

Another school of thought, the neo-classical school, argues that there is no money illusion, and that if prices rise as the result of an expansion of the money supply the demand for wages increases in line with prices. Thus there is no short-term reduction in unemployment following an expansion of the money supply.

The Maintenance of a Favourable Balance of Payments.

During the late 1970's and early 1980's Britain's oil surplus was a problem for governments. It resulted in the increase of imported industrial goods which reduced domestic production, and to an over-investment in sterling which increased the cost of exports. Governments can reduce a balance of payments surplus in one of the following ways. Firstly, the government can inflate the economy, which will have the added benefit of reducing the cost of imports. Secondly, the government can revalue the domestic currency which will also make imports cheaper and push up the price of exports, thus reducing the surplus.

In the case of a balance of payments deficit, a number of options are available to a government. A short-term deficit can be met by calling on reserves, increasing the amount of government borrowing, or raising interest rates. The following policies can be used to cure a longer-term balance of payments deficit. Firstly, the government may reduce the demand for imports through fiscal or monetary controls, thus avoiding the need to erect barriers to trade which might be regarded as protectionist by trading partners. Secondly, when the balance of payments deficit is due to a deficit in the capital account the government may encourage the inflow of foreign capital by raising interest rates, or discourage the out-flow of domestic capital by instituting a measure of exchange control.

The Promotion of Economic Growth.

Economic growth is the result of a real, as opposed to a nominal, increase in Gross Domestic Product. The rate of growth of GDP per capita is affected by changes in the population level; an increase in population that is greater than the increase in GDP will result in a declining GDP per capita. The rate of economic growth of a nation is not, by itself, an indication of whether average living standards have increased. The economist is therefore interested in knowing how income is distributed throughout the population.

After the Second World War government policies aimed at stimulating the growth of the economy were predominantly aimed at demand management. A programme of nationalisation in the late 1940's and 1950's brought many of the most important industries under government control, when it was felt that central planning would best advance economic growth. This policy has been largely revised since 1979, however, and the 'privatisation programme' of the Conservative government returned many of the former nationalised industries to the private sector. Growth management since that date has been predominantly concerned with supply, and has taken the following forms:

- Reductions in income tax to stimulate saving and investment.
- Control of the money supply to keep inflation down.

Summary

1) Direct taxation consists of income tax payable on personal incomes, corporation tax payable on company profits, and taxes payable on the transfer of capital. Indirect taxation consists of Value Added Tax, and customs and excise duties.

2) Cyclical unemployment occurs when there is a general deficiency of demand due to a trade depression. Frictional employment occurs when labour cannot be transferred easily from one form of production to another.

3) Government action to reduce a balance of payments surplus may take the form of inflating the economy, or revaluing the domestic currency. Action to rectify a balance of payments deficit includes the use of fiscal or monetary controls, or in the case of a deficit in the capital account, manipulation of the interest rate or the introduction of exchange controls.

Self-Assessment Test Eleven – Questions

1) What are the three ways in which governments implement their policy objectives?

2) Define
   a) cyclical unemployment

   b) frictional unemployment

3) What is meant by the 'money illusion'?

Self-Assessment Test Eleven – Answers

1) a) taxation and government spending

b) monetary policy

c) direct intervention

2) a) general deficiency of demand due to a trade depression

b) labour is not easily transferable between different forms of production.

3) the tendency of people to assume that an increase in money wages is equivalent to an increase in real wages.

Past Examination Questions on These Topics.

1) What are the principal objectives of macro-economic policy? Why do governments face such difficulties in achieving all these objectives?

2) Explain how a change in government expenditure on goods and services and a change in taxation can each separately be used to deflate the economy. What considerations should influence the choice between these deflationary measures?

3) Describe what you consider to be the chief objectives of government policy affecting the economy as a whole. To what extent do these conflict with one another?

4) Outline four possible ways in which taxation can be used as an instrument of government policy.

5) In what ways may the government attempt to correct an unfavourable balance of payments?

6) Discuss the methods which may be used by the government to correct an unfavourable balance of payments.

7) 'The macroeconomic objectives of government may not always be mutually compatible.' Identify and explain the possible conflicts which may arise.

8) Taxation can serve many functions in addition to raising revenue. Discuss these additional functions in relation to the system of taxation in your country.